LONDON

A CENTURY IN THE CITY

St Paul's Churchyard and Ludgate Hill from St Paul's Cathedral, *c.*1880. While St Paul's has presented an unchanging face to the City for nearly 300 years, the cathedral's setting has changed and evolved, with the original plain but elegant seventeenth and eighteenth-century buildings of the City's post-Great Fire rebuilding giving way to the more ornate styles of the Victorian age. Examples of these can be seen to the left, but to the right the earlier styles prevailed for the time being, these ones housing Messrs Griffith & Farren, the booksellers and the offices of the London & General Plate Glass Insurance Co. A replacement office block would shortly arise but its handsome lines would be obscured by the gigantic white-letter advertising of Goodman the dentist who occupied it. The same corner was taken in the 1960s for the controversial Juxon House which partly blocked some views of St Paul's, but yet another new block has since restored some dignity to the cathedral's precinct. To the left of the picture are the shop and warehouse of Messrs Dakin, tea merchants – their sharply angled corner would shortly be rounded off through road widening. Further along, the street runs downhill into the valley of the river Fleet, passing the site of Ludgate, once an entry point in the City's Roman and medieval defensive wall. Wren's St Paul's Cathedral was completed in 1712, and to mark the event, a statue was erected of the reigning monarch, Queen Anne, centre.

LONDON

A CENTURY IN THE CITY

BRIAN GIRLING

TEMPUS

Cover picture: The Bank of England, *c.* 1895. The bank is seen long before the lofty additions of 1925-39 were erected within the eighteenth-century outer walls.

First published 2007

Tempus Publishing
Cirencester Road, Chalford,
Stroud, Gloucestershire, GL6 8PE
www.tempus-publishing.com

Tempus Publishing is an imprint of NPI Media Group

British Library Cataloguing in Publication Data.
A catalogue record for this book is available from the British Library.

ISBN 978 0 7524 4507 6

Typesetting and origination by NPI Media Group
Printed in Great Britain

CONTENTS

Bishopsgate Station, c.1865. The 1830s and 1840s saw the beginnings of the great railway building era in London, but the first stations to serve the City were located outside its boundaries: London Bridge opened in 1836, Minories in 1840 and the grandiose 'London' station also in 1840. Renamed 'Bishopsgate' in 1846, the old London Station handled City-bound passengers from East Anglia on the Eastern Counties Railway (later the Great Eastern Railway), until the lines were extended into a new terminus in the City, Liverpool Street, which opened in 1874. Bishopsgate was then rebuilt as a rail freight terminal until a fire ended its activities in 1964.

ACKNOWLEDGEMENTS

I would like to thank London Metropolitan Archives and D.A. Jones (London Trolleybus Preservation Society) for their kindness in allowing the reproduction of copyright material in this book. A big 'thank you' is also due to Guildhall Library and London Metropolitan Archives whose helpful staff and excellent facilities have, as ever, proved invaluable.

Books consulted include: *The Buildings of England, London Vol. 1, The City of London*, Simon Bradley and Nikolaus Pevsner; *The City of London Book*, Richard Tames; *Streets of the City*, Judy Pulley; *Images of the City of London*, Warren Grynberg; *The Visitors Guide to the City of London Churches*, Tony Tucker.

INTRODUCTION

Twenty centuries have gone into the making of the London we know today, each of them leaving a little of itself for those who followed to build on. At the centre of this vast metropolis is the ancient nucleus where it all began in the first century AD when the first Londoners were Romans. They called their outpost of the Roman Empire 'Londinium' – it is now the City of London, the famous 'Square Mile'.

In the present day the skyline glitters with the great commercial towers of this global powerhouse of a city, yet in the labyrinth of streets, which for the most part still follow a medieval pattern, there are world-renowned buildings and ancient treasures which have survived as the City evolved and modernised.

Utilising rare and unseen photographs, including haunting images from the mid-nineteenth century, the following pages offer an exploration and celebration of the City through a century (and a little more) from the 1850s to the 1960s beginning at a time when the City's resident population was declining but its status as a world city and port at the heart of a global empire was growing even greater.

Some of the photographs recall the old City docks which brought trade and prosperity before these facilities relocated further downstream. Other images explore shady lanes and teeming streets where the day-to-day life of the City was enacted and where a host of shops, markets and refreshment houses was on hand to cater for City folk including the daily influx of City workers and business people. There is a look at the historic neighbourhoods around one of the greatest English cathedrals, St Paul's, and the Blitz of the 1940s which laid waste swathes of the City including part of its remarkable heritage of ancient parish churches.

Some of the traditions and ceremonies which are unique to the City are recalled, as are the great royal events and processions which the City embraces with colourful enthusiasm. Also pictured are historic sites beside the Thames which the mid-nineteenth century transport revolution transformed into new stations and bridges for the railway age, while ambitious road-building schemes attempted to ease the City's eternal horse-drawn traffic jams. As the pictures show, the age of the horse merged into that of the motor but the jams remained. Early photographs reveal how the fabric of the City was changing; around four in every five City buildings were rebuilt between 1850 and 1900.

Rare colour pictures also remind us that the Victorian and Edwardian City was not a place of grey and sepia monochrome but was as colourful and vibrant as it is in the present day. In the City, as well as elsewhere, we may mourn the passing of that which was familiar to us, but perhaps this book will revive a half-forgotten memory or intrigue us with fading images of times we never knew in a City which is known and loved worldwide.

THE MARITIME CITY

The Upper Pool of London from London Bridge, c. 1895. This is where London began nearly 2,000 years ago when occupying Roman forces founded a settlement beside the great tidal river they called Tamesis. By bridging the river at this point, Roman Londinium achieved strategic importance and prosperity through maritime trade for which it was ideally situated with the estuary facing the great continental river systems across the North Sea. Through the fluctuating fortunes of succeeding centuries the docks expanded far downstream and evolved into the world's greatest centre of maritime trade, the Port of London. The point at which it all began is seen here in its Victorian heyday when, such was the press of shipping waiting to use the docking facilities, many vessels had to moor far from the shore. As the twentieth century progressed, containerisation triggered the demise of the old City and East End docks, and the river's other role as an amenity for leisure and tourism became increasingly dominant.

Testing Tower Bridge, 1894. As London and its port expanded through the nineteenth century it became increasingly vital for the burgeoning dockland-generated road traffic to have another Thames crossing below London Bridge without impeding the constant stream of vessels accessing the City's wharves. Victorian technology finally found a spectacular solution to the problem by reviving and updating a feature once used on the medieval London Bridge where a drawbridge could be raised to let larger ships through. When Tower Bridge opened in 1894, its twin bascules carrying the roadway could be raised whenever a large vessel required passage upstream. In the last days before the bridge's official opening by Edward, Prince of Wales, the stability of the bascules was tested to ensure the structure could withstand the heaviest weights likely to be imposed upon it. The picture shows the testing process underway with ballast-laden wagons and heavy road rollers drawn up at the extremity of the southern bascule. Over a century on, this most iconic of London landmarks copes well with the demands of modern traffic.

Tower Bridge from Bermondsey, 1894. It took eight years to build the bridge after which pedestrians were at last able to make the new crossing. As seen here, the approach road had yet to receive its granite-sett paving; wooden paving blocks were used on the moveable bascules to lessen the weight.

Tower Bridge from The Wharf, Tower of London, c. 1912. Londoners and visitors were quick to appreciate the magnificence of the new bridge which soon became an international symbol of London. Designed by City architect, Sir Horace Jones, the bridge's Gothic architecture complements that of its ancient neighbour, the Tower of London.

The Upper Pool of London from Tower Bridge, *c.* 1903. Pedestrians not wishing to undergo the frequent delays caused by the raising of the bridge's bascules had the option of crossing the river by high-level walkways. The exertions this involved were rewarded by panoramic river views running towards the classical Custom House, left centre, a building from 1812-17 and the last in a succession of Custom Houses dating from the fourteenth century. Adjacent was London's wholesale fish market, Billingsgate, and nearer the camera, ancient Tower Hill and its massive Victorian bonded warehouses.

The Tower of London from Tower Hill, *c.* 1905. Almost 1,000 years of turbulent and often bloody history are encapsulated within the formidable walls of the fortress and palace begun by William the Conqueror around 1077 to secure the eastern river approaches to London. The Tower was built along the line of an even earlier fortification, the great wall which encircled Roman Londinium. In the foreground Tower Hill, once the scene of many an execution, was a useful pull-up for cabbies and wagon drivers.

Above: Guard Mounting Parade (2nd Lincolns), Tower of London, *c.* 1905. Palace, prison, menagerie and Royal Mint; these were some of the varied roles undertaken by the Tower during its lengthy history, but it was built as a fortress and a military presence has remained ever since. Seen here are Waterloo Barracks, which were built in 1845 and could accommodate 1,000 soldiers. In the background is the chapel of St Peter ad Vincula, whose records can be traced back to 1130 when it was a parish church of the City standing outside the Tower's walls – it remains a place of worship for the Tower's resident community.

Left: At home in the Tower of London, *c.* 1908. Among those who live permanently in the Tower's precincts are its yeoman warders, whose houses and apartments are located in various parts of the ancient complex. Seen here outside his home at No. 8 The Parade, which faces tower Green, is Yeoman Warder William Battman who fulfilled his duties from 1896 to 1918.

Above: Fishing boats off Billingsgate, *c.* 1895. Billingsgate has been an important landing place on the Thames since Saxon times, but its more familiar role as London's fish market began late in the seventeenth century. A succession of market buildings culminated in 1878 in the structure we see today to designs by Sir Horace Jones, the architect of Tower Bridge.

Below: A good catch of herring, Billingsgate Market, Lower Thames Street by Custom House, *c.* 1900. An image by local photographer Joseph Neil of St Dunstan's Hill pictures a lively scene as the fish, liberally mixed with ice, is prepared for an onward journey by road. Billingsgate's activities relocated to East London in 1982, thus ending a richly aromatic slice of City life.

A 'Belle' paddle steamer at London Bridge Wharf, *c.* 1900. The popularity of the Thames as a maritime highway to riverside towns and coastal resorts is revealed here with a well-laden steamer picking up passengers by London Bridge. To the left is the hall of The Worshipful Company of Fishmongers, while the tower is that of St Magnus the Martyr (begun 1668), which stood directly on the approach to old London Bridge before Rennie's bridge (1831) took the crossing a short distance upstream.

London Bridge, *c.* 1947. With its taller, wider spans, the bridge designed by Rennie cleared the river of the obstruction to shipping presented by the medieval London Bridge of 1209 and its even earlier predecessors. Rennie's bridge is seen here against a war-ravaged riverside where clearances have opened up a temporary view of Upper Thames Street.

The future site of Cannon Street Station and bridge, c. 1862. The 1860s was a decade marked by great engineering projects in the Square Mile as new roads and railways began to change the face of what was still an essentially Georgian city. It was in the 1860s that London's expanding railway network bridged the Thames into the City for the first time, initially at Blackfriars (1862) followed by Cannon Street where a new City terminus was built from 1865-66 for the South Eastern Railway. The site chosen was that of the former Hanseatic Merchant's Steelyard where for 600 years from the thirteenth century, a self-governing enclave of some 400 German merchants lived peacefully on land given to them by Henry III. The last of the old steelyard can be seen in the picture but the station's lofty flanking walls and towers would soon arise. The railway bridge serving the station was initially called the Alexandra Bridge after the then Princess of Wales (Queen Alexandra from 1901). A tiny remnant of this long-lost view still exists in Cousin Lane Stairs, an old access point to the Thames foreshore, while Steelyard Passage, a tunnel which carries the modern Thames Path beneath the station perpetuates this old name. At the far right of the picture are the City of London Brewery's new buildings (1862) which would survive until 1941.

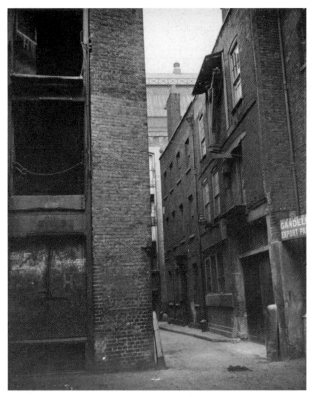

Greenwich Street by Red Lion Wharf, *c.* 1919. In the hinterland behind the riverside wharves, a densely packed maze of narrow lanes and alleys ran inland to Upper Thames Street. The street pattern was still that of medieval London despite the destruction wrought by the Great Fire in 1666, but that would change with post-war clearance and rebuilding. Greenwich Street typified this quarter of the City with small warehouses and run-down but still elegant post-Fire houses which had been put to a variety of uses, mostly connected with the maritime trade. Part of Cannon Street Station is visible here.

Brickhill Lane with Red Lion Wharf and Three Cranes Wharf, *c.* 1919. The lane with its old warehouses and workshops was an atmospheric survivor of the old port and included the premises of Henry Hill & Sons, quill merchants and sealing-wax makers, and Vintry Ward School which was instituted in 1710 (rebuilt 1840). The school was a reminder of a once more residential City in the past centuries.

No. 1, Cousin Lane, Upper Thames Street, *c.* 1919. Building land in the City is elusive and expensive but here is an example of how Victorian builders maximised the potential of a seemingly impossible site. This slimmest of buildings separated two historic passages to the Thames, Cousin Lane, left and Dowgate Dock, right, where a narrow inlet of the river existed close to the now hidden Walbrook stream.

Dowgate Dock, *c.* 1919. The history of this narrowest of Thames inlets can be traced back to Saxon times when there was a Watergate in the wall which then ran along the riverside. An open quay to the right lasted into the nineteenth century but this was later sacrificed for warehouse building.

Queenhithe, Bull Wharf and Kennet Wharf from Southwark Bridge, c. 1858. Known in Saxon times as Aetheredeshyth, Queenhithe's deeply recessed harbour (left) was a popular landing point on the river, but its location above medieval London Bridge rendered it inaccessible to larger ships after the bridge's drawbridge fell out of use early in the 1600s. In the 1850s the riverside here still looked much as it had done in the 1700s with a tree-shaded dock and quays lined by elegant post-Fire houses. One of these, No. 13 Queenhithe, housed the picturesque King's Arms pub. These old terraces were nearing the end of their lives and soon a wave of Victorian warehouse building would transform the waterfront – the King's Arms site was about to be reborn as the lofty Smith's Wharf. Hard by Queenhithe's harbour was a wooden slipway where small boats were hauled up onto the quayside, and to its right was Bull Wharf where goods were 'lightered, landed and housed'. Its ramshackle sheds would soon be replaced by a new Bull Wharf, another of the warehouse blocks which would characterise this part of the City. Also seen here are the premises of William Rose, lead & varnish manufacturers (centre), and Kennet Wharf with its iron founders and wharfingers.

In the distance, St Paul's Cathedral looks down on the low-rise City of the 1850s from which Wren's churches still rise above the rooftops. St Mary Somerset is to the left with St Michael's Queenhithe on the right. The latter was notable for its stepped steeple and weathervane in the shape of a ship – the church was demolished in 1876.

Above: The rebuilding of Southwark Bridge seen from Queenhithe, *c.* 1919. The first Southwark Bridge was built from 1814–19 in response to calls for a new river crossing between the two City bridges at Blackfriars and London Bridge, and was constructed of iron to the designs of Rennie. Although highly regarded, the earlier bridge was replaced by a new crossing which opened in 1921.

Right: Blackfriars Bridge from Queenhithe and Brook's Wharf, *c.* 1919. Before the City's riverside walkways were built in modern times, this was one of the few places along the City shore where it was possible to catch a glimpse of the river. Life on the Thames and in docks like Queenhithe was ruled by the state of the tide – at low water the docks were inaccessible to shipping and mud flats were exposed along the foreshore.

Queen Victoria Street and Upper Thames Street, Blackfriars, *c.* 1920. Two worlds met here; to the left the stone-fronted grandeur of Queen Victoria Street (1871), and to the right the maritime world of Upper Thames Street where the street and its forerunners have followed the course of the river for nearly 2,000 years. This was a world of blackened warehouses and dark narrow lanes running down to the river, much of it built on land reclaimed from the Thames. In Norman times, Castle Baynard, a defensive fortress for the western City stood near here – the name lives on as a ward of the City of London. The picture preserves a typically busy scene and includes a white-coated street orderly clearing up the deposits of the area's large horse population. In the middle distance is Puddle Dock and beside it the towering City Mills Building (1850) whose lofty chimney once overshadowed the area. When milling ceased here the building was used as a tin-plate works and warehouse before war damage removed its upper floors. It was here that the late Lord Miles realised his vision of bringing live theatre to the City with the opening in 1959 of the renowned Mermaid Theatre. Today this scene is a world of relentless traffic and disgracefully drab office buildings.

Opposite above: The Mermaid Theatre, Upper Thames Street, *c.* 1959. In the 1850s this was the tallest commercial block on the City's riverfront, but a century later and with its stature much reduced by war damage, it was reborn as the Mermaid Theatre. The building's origins were evident to theatregoers passing through the original cast-iron columned entrance into an auditorium walled in Victorian warehouse brick. Remnants of Blackfriars' maritime past linger in the picture and Puddle Dock, right, had yet to be infilled.

Right: Puddle Dock, Blackfriars, *c.* 1920. This was another of the river's tidal inlets which gave barges and lighters a safe haven away from the fast-flowing currents of the main stream. In medieval times it was a place where horses were watered but Puddle Dock achieved fame when the Mermaid Theatre was created out of the buildings seen on the left. With the infilling of the dock and further reclamation of land from the river for a new road system and riverside walk, Puddle Dock is now a busy highway.

The site of the first Blackfriars railway bridge, *c.* 1856. Pockets of small-scale industry existed along the old City waterfront, the only building of any stature being City Mills, by Puddle Dock, right. Seen here at St Ann's Wharf are the modest premises of iron founders F.A. Tiddeman & Co., and Thomas Perry & Sons, while Blackfriars Wharf accommodated coal merchant T. Freeman. Lime and chalk merchant William Lee traded from premises which ran back from the river to long-lost Earl Street, but Franz Steigerwall, 'foreign glass manufacturer' enjoyed the bow-windowed elegance of No. 1 Chatham Place, left.

Chatham Place was once a residential street at the approach to old Blackfriars Bridge. This part of the riverfront would disappear in 1862 and be replaced by a bridge carrying the lines of the London, Chatham and Dover Railway across the river to a terminus by Ludgate Hill which would open in 1864. St Paul's Station (later Blackfriars) opened in 1886 together with a parallel railway bridge.

Here, the church of St Andrew-by-the-Wardrobe appears in front of the ever dominant St Paul's Cathedral.

Blackfriars Bridge, *c.* 1928. For centuries London Bridge was the City's only river crossing but in 1769 it was joined by Blackfriars Bridge, a stone-built structure designed by Robert Mylne. Usefully serving the western City, Mylne's bridge lasted a century, but with tidal scouring weakening its supports it was decided to rebuild. A new cast-iron bridge was opened by Queen Victoria in 1869 and by 1910 the crossing had been widened to take electric tram lines. These became important links in London's burgeoning tramway system allowing a loop line to connect with Westminster Bridge via Victoria Embankment. Lasting until 1952, this was the only place in the City of London where a through tram service was allowed to operate. The latticed structure on the left was the first of Blackfriars' pair of railway bridges, the site of which is seen in the preceding photograph. That bridge fell out of use, and although its superstructure was removed in 1985, its massive supporting columns continue their progress across the Thames to this day making one of the oddest sights on the river. The second Blackfriars Bridge (obscured here) opened in 1886.

Land reclamation for Victoria Embankment, 1860s. Before the 1860s, much of London's river was hidden away behind docks, wharves and other private property, its waters only visible to the average Londoner from the bridges or the flights of stairs which gave access to the foreshore at low tide. In one of the greatest civil engineering projects in London during the 1860s a length of the Thames was opened up for all to enjoy by the building of a great riverside boulevard running from Westminster Bridge and entering the City by the Temple, before linking up with the then new Queen Victoria Street at Blackfriars. The project was conceived by the Metropolitan Board of Works' chief engineer Sir Joseph Bazalgette and involved the reclamation of around thirty acres of land from the river, here at its widest in central London. The work, which included the provision of a new sewerage system, began in 1862 and was completed by 1868 only for the carriageways to be dug up again for the building of the District Railway's Underground line beneath the road. Victoria Embankment officially opened on 13 July 1870, preceded on 30 May by the railway, whose lines ran beneath what had a decade earlier been the waters of the Thames at high tide. The new road was the widest in the City and usefully relieved congestion in Fleet Street and Strand in Westminster. The works seen here ran up to Blackfriars Bridge where there was a temporary crossing in use from 1863-69. This was sophisticated enough to feature gas lighting for its walkway but it disappeared with the opening of the new permanent bridge by Queen Victoria on 6 November 1869.

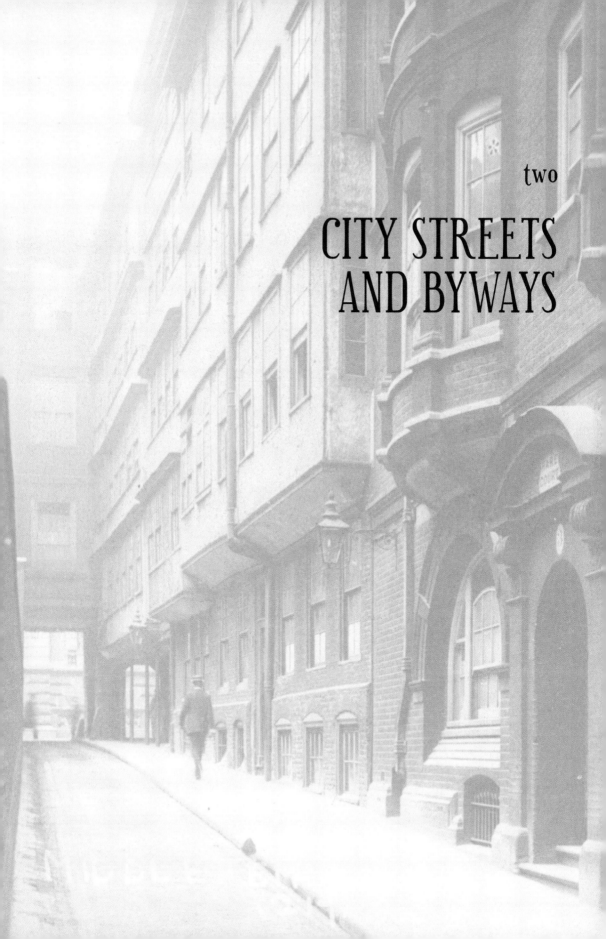

two

CITY STREETS
AND BYWAYS

Crutched Friars from New London Street, *c.* 1912. Although the City of the twenty-first century presents a modern face to the world, it does not take long to find plentiful clues to its true antiquity. Despite the loss of many streets and byways through the centuries, there is still a network of historic lanes, alleys and courts which continue to follow the pattern of medieval times and retain names which evoke a vivid sense of the life and topography of the City in past centuries.

Many of the street names are unique to the City including Crutched Friars where the Friary of the Holy Cross stood from *c.*1298. The friars wore habits emblazoned with a cross and the street name derived from the 'crossed friars' who were seen hereabouts. To the right of the picture are the soot-blackened walls of St Olave, Hart Street, a medieval church where stonework from around 1270 can still be seen. Samuel Pepys, the diarist whose vivid word pictures of City life in the mid-1600s are still avidly read, is buried in the church. Beyond is Seething Lane and the Globe pub which was replaced by the handsome Walsingham House in 1929, and there is a distant view of Fenchurch Street Station. Despite some grim 1960s office buildings, there are still some fine Georgian survivals close by including the highly atmospheric French Ordinary Court, a dark and cavernous cul-de-sac beneath Fenchurch Street Station. (Courtesy of City of London, London Metropolitan Archives).

Aldgate High Street from Minories, c. 1913. Named after a gate (demolished 1761) in the City's old defensive wall, this was the principal route into the City from Roman Camulodunum (Colchester) and other parts of East Anglia. The street was for centuries thronged with horse-drawn traffic entering and leaving the City, but here modernity was catching up with motor buses and a pair of Underground stations; Aldgate (1876) and Aldgate East (1884), while in the background, electric trams ran to the City boundary. Post-war rebuilding has given this old street of coaching inns and small shops a drab new face of overbearing office blocks and pedestrian subways.

Aldgate Pump, c. 1905. The origins of Aldgate's well can be traced back to the thirteenth century when it was located just inside the City wall, but here the mainly Victorian pump had been moved for street widening. To the right is St Katherine Cree, Leadenhall Street, a church rebuilt from 1628-31 and a precious survivor of the Great Fire and the Blitz.

Above: Fenchurch Street by Church Row (St Katherine's Row), *c.* 1920. This was part of the Roman route into the City from Aldgate, but it is more famous today for its railway station. Church Row, right, led to the church of St Katherine Coleman (1740) which was demolished in 1926. Its churchyard is still here as is the early nineteenth century East India Arms, right.

Left: Catherine Court, *c.* 1911. Grand building schemes in the City often bring landmark structures but part of the neighbourhood's visible history can be lost in the process. This elegant gated close of houses from around 1725 was sacrificed for the mighty Port of London Authority development of 1912–22 when a network of historic streets and byways disappeared. Catherine Court was once a quiet residential enclave, but as the City's population declined the houses were given over to office use.

Fish Street Hill, *c.* 1880. The steep narrow street was, for centuries, the principal approach route to old London Bridge before King William Street and a new bridge were opened in 1831. The dominant feature here is the 202ft tall Monument, Wren's grand commemoration of the City's worst disaster, the Great Fire of 1666 – the height of the column is equidistant to the seat of the Fire, Farynor's bakehouse in Pudding Lane. To the left of the picture a gap in the houses by the Monument Tavern marks the churchyard of St Leonard Eastcheap, one of the first of the churches to be destroyed in the Fire. It was not rebuilt, but its churchyard lingered on only to be built over in the late 1800s. Another Fire casualty was St Margaret, Fish Street Hill – a City Corporation plaque records its site by the Monument.

Above: Eastcheap by Philpot Lane, *c.* 1910. From Saxon times, Eastcheap served the east of the City as its principal market place with butchers' stalls predominating. The name of one of Eastcheap's side turnings, Pudding Lane, referred to the offal which was taken that way for disposal in the Thames. The picture is of a less grisly scene with the typically varied façades of Victorian business houses with Eastcheap Post Office on the Philpot Lane corner.

Left: Philpot Lane from Eastcheap, *c.* 1918. The street bears the name of former resident Sir John Philpot, Alderman of Langbourne Ward and Lord Mayor of London in 1378. In 1918 the street contained the usual City mixture of shops and business houses – the premises on the right provided office accommodation for over sixty businesses. Passers-by may have been tempted by the shops which offered cups of cocoa for 1d, shaves for 2d and haircuts for 4d.

Above: King William Street from Adelaide Place, *c.* 1928. These streets were laid out to give access to the new and resited London Bridge of 1831 and bypass the old route via Fish Street Hill and its chaotic crossroads at Lower Thames Street. The new roads ran above Upper and Lower Thames Streets and were effectively the City's first flyover – one of the parapets is seen on the right.

Right: Love Lane (Lovat Lane), *c.* 1909. The steep slopes running down to Lower Thames Street were once part of the riverbank before land reclamation through the centuries took the river further away. The medieval lanes hereabouts were devastated in the Fire, but following the City's subsequent rebuilding, its great architect Sir Christopher Wren occupied a mansion sited to the right of the picture (see *City of London*, Tempus, 1998). Here a new office building had just arisen on its site.

The Royal Exchange, *c.* 1858. The heart of the City is suitably grand and is distinguished by its trio of great neo-classical buildings; the Bank of England, Mansion House and the Royal Exchange, which was created as a meeting place for City merchants to conduct their business. The original Exchange opened in 1566 and was called Gresham's Exchange after its founder, Sir Thomas Gresham. A new Exchange opened in 1671 followed by the building seen here which was opened by Queen Victoria in 1844. Still quite new at the time of this photograph, the Royal Exchange overlooks its forecourt where fashionably dressed City gentlemen of the day sported tall top hats and ladies the voluminous crinoline.

The convergence of some of the City's busiest streets often resulted in gridlock traffic although it looks peaceful enough here. The horse omnibus represented what was for London a fairly recent transport innovation – the first buses had appeared some thirty years earlier.

Lothbury leading to Gresham Street, *c.* 1928. With the Bank of England behind the camera and the dark granite-faced splendour of the Northern Assurance Building on the right, Lothbury is at the City's financial heartland. Gresham Street originated in the 1840s when four ancient lanes were widened and linked into a single street bearing the name of the founder of the Royal Exchange.

Cannon Street, *c.* 1912. Of Roman origin, this was called Candlewick Street in the thirteenth century after the candle makers and tallow chandlers who traded here. Their legacy is perpetuated by Candlewick, the ward of the City through which Cannon Street continues to run. The medieval thoroughfare ran as far west as Walbrook, but in 1854 the widening and rebuilding of a run of narrow congested lanes gave the City a fine new street which brought Cannon Street to St Paul's Churchyard.

Mansion House, *c.* 1870. The official residence of the Lord Mayor of London since 1752 is seen at a time when the construction of Queen Victoria Street was giving Mansion House a new setting. Empty sites still abounded but in 1873 there would be a new neighbour, the National Safe Deposit Building, now the City of London Magistrates' Court.

Sunday morning in the City, Mansion House, *c.* 1880. Sometimes a place of equine gridlock, this was once dubbed 'the busiest road junction in the world', but on a Sunday morning with everything closed for the weekend, it can be as tranquil a place as could be desired. Mansion House, left, presides over it all while further along, Queen Victoria Street and Poultry are separated by the ornate rounded corner of the Mappin & Webb building (1871) which would be lost despite a spirited campaign for its preservation in the 1980s and 1990s. Poultry's name recalls the medieval poulterers who traded here, while to the right, the European Tavern inhabits an early post-Fire building in Mansion House Street, the shortest main street in the City. Grand stone-fronted financial houses would soon take the Tavern's site and that of the Azienda Insurance building on the Princes Street corner.

Lombard Street by Birchin Lane and Change Alley, 1902. Here is more of bankers' London with venerable financial houses lining a street settled in the fourteenth century by Italian financiers from Lombardy who bequeathed a street name and an enduring financial legacy. The street is given distinction by its ornate bank signs, banned during the reign of Charles II but revived here in 1902.

Cheapside from St Paul's Churchyard, *c.* 1889. In medieval times this was West Cheap, the 'western market' and a principal source of household essentials for the City's then considerable population. Here the street has small-scale commercial premises including, left, the Abyssinian Gold Co. and Wilcox & Gibbs, who sold sewing machines. To the right, the Cathedral Hotel stands by Old Change, a narrow street which would be lost in the Blitz.

Roadworks in Cheapside, *c.* 1906. The eternal bane of town life has closed the street but the routine of Cheapside continues as best it can. In the background is Cheapside's great landmark, St Mary-le-Bow, Wren's rebuilding of a church who's history spans a millennium. The remarkable steeple containing the legendary 'Bow Bells' rises high above an eleventh-century crypt and the remains of a Roman pavement.

Queen Victoria Street by Watling Street and Queen Street, *c.* 1901. Just thirty years old when photographed here, the street has already matured into a fine City thoroughfare with impressive ranges of commercial premises. Queen Street, centre left, was built following the Great Fire but to the left, Watling Street, the 'Aethelingstrate' of the thirteenth century, represented the traditional east/west route hereabouts. Behind the camera, evidence of the London of the third century would be revealed in 1954 when excavations uncovered the remains of a Roman mithraic temple.

Queen Victoria Street, *c.* 1920. A heavy load of paper makes its way towards the presses of Fleet Street against a backdrop of the *Times* building. The creation of the new Queen Victoria Street gave *The Thunderer* the opportunity in 1874 to establish its new headquarters close to the newspaper's original premises in Printing House Square.

The Fleet Valley, *c.* 1858. From his viewpoint on the tower of St Andrew's church, Holborn, the photographer looks out over one of the places where the outlines of the ancient landscape upon which the City evolved can still be discerned. In the millennia before the Roman occupation this was a green valley through which a clear stream ran to the great river to the south. The lower reaches of the stream were substantial enough to be navigable and there was a tidal creek at its southern end. The Saxons later knew the stream as 'Fleota' (Fleet) while upstream reaches were called 'Holebourne' from which the name Holborn derived. Increasing population and commercial activity brought pollution and the lower Fleet degenerated into a sewer but from 1734-37 the Fleet was culverted and a new street, Farringdon Street, built above it together with Fleet Market, a double row of single-storey shops. Farringdon Street can be seen running from left to right in the picture with, bottom right, part of Farringdon market which was established for the sale of fruit and vegetables following the closure of Fleet Market in 1828 – it later removed to a site by Charterhouse Street. A tall chimney marks the presence of Messrs Pontifex, brass and coppersmiths who would still be here into the twentieth century. The low-rise City of the 1850s is well caught here with narrow shadowy side streets running into Farringdon Street. The names of two of them, Newcastle Street and Seacoal Lane, are reminders of the quays beside the Fleet where barges once discharged their cargoes of coal – these had been brought by sea to the Thames from Newcastle.

Holborn Viaduct, Farringdon Street, *c.* 1910. For centuries east/west traffic in the north of the City struggled to negotiate the steep slippery streets into and out of the Fleet Valley. All that changed on 8 November 1869 when Queen Victoria opened Holborn Viaduct which at last gave the traffic a level run across the valley. Mostly hidden by buildings, the viaduct reveals itself at Shoe Lane and here, where the photographer has pictured a lively scene.

Farringdon Street from Ludgate Circus, *c.* 1905. This is the site of Fleet Bridge where the highway from Westminster crossed the Fleet's waters *en route* for St Paul's Cathedral. Replacing the river with busy Farringdon Street created a congested crossroads, but from 1864-69 the building of the circus's quadrants eased the traffic flow. The large neo-Gothic pile in the distance is the Congregational Memorial Hall which arose in 1875 on the site of the notorious Fleet Prison. The Fleet had accommodated countless numbers of the City's ne'er-do-wells from its openings in the 1100s to closure in 1842.

Fleet Street by Chancery Lane, *c.* 1905. Fleet Street's name will forever be associated with the worlds of journalism and publishing even though the vast numbers of newspapers and periodicals which were based here have moved away. The first of London's daily newspapers, the *Daily Courant*, began publishing from Ludgate Hill in 1702 but it was the 1800s before newspaper production began to dominate the Ludgate end of Fleet Street itself. The 1920s and 1930s saw several national dailies build grand headquarters buildings for themselves – these remain having since been put to other uses. The part of Fleet Street seen here is where the journalists' London of old merges with lawyers' London. The City's western reaches are almost exclusively the preserve of the legal profession and of the mellow precincts of barristers' chambers which are a world apart form the busy streets which border them. With the Royal Courts of Justice behind the camera, Chancery Lane, left, accommodates the Law Society's Hall and a variety of atmospheric shops which cater to the legal profession. To the right, a series of passages and lanes are access points of Inner and Middle Temple, a mellow precinct of the legal profession since the fourteenth century when lawyers began to inhabit premises vacated by the Knights Templar, a religious order which had itself moved here around 1160. An old house overhanging the pavement, right, is a rare survival of the Great Fire and is known today as Prince Henry's Room. Dating from 1611, the building began life as an inn, the Prince's Arms, before going on to house a waxworks and as seen here, a hairdresser. Restoration in 1905 created the fine timbered frontage we know today. The photograph is contemporary with the setting up in a neighbouring building of the first office of the Automobile Association, but for the time being the horse continues to rule the roads.

Opposite above: From a bus top, Ludgate Circus, *c.* 1912. The motor age starts to take hold in the City with motor-buses and taxis beginning to consign their horse-drawn forebears to history. Electric advertising signs brought a touch of the West End to the City, while the railway bridge (1865) was a controversial feature until its removal in 1990.

Opposite below: Fleet Street by Shoe Lane, *c.* 1911. *Ideas*, a weekly illustrated magazine, has attracted an assortment of City types with its windows full of news pictures. The scene would be transformed in 1933 when the *Daily Express* built an eye-catching headquarters building faced in black glass and chromium strips.

Left: Temple Bar, Fleet Street, *c.* 1870. The entry point into the City from Westminster was marked in style by Wren's elegant gate which was built in 1672 following the Great Fire. Earlier structures had included a small gate topped by a prison and in the fourteenth century a chain across the road. As traffic levels increased the gate was deemed an impediment and was removed in 1878 to spend the next century in exile at a Hertfordshire mansion. The year 2004 saw the return of the restored Temple Bar to the City where it makes a fine entrance to a remodelled Paternoster Square adjacent to Wren's greatest work, St Paul's Cathedral.

Left: Temple Bar, February 1872. Once adorned with the heads of executed traitors, the decorations here are for a Royal visit to the City when Queen Victoria and other members of the Royal Family attended a Service of Thanksgiving at St Paul's Cathedral for the recovery of the Prince of Wales (later Edward VII) from a life-threatening illness. The Royal carriage procession rode from Buckingham Palace until, in accordance with tradition, it was confronted by closed gates at Temple Bar. In an act of allegiance, the sovereign was then presented with the City Sword, the gates opened and the procession continued.

Opposite: Middle Temple Lane off Fleet Street, *c.* 1905. These buildings still give a rare taste of how a typical City byway would have looked in the decades before much of it was lost to the Great Fire in 1666. Post-Fire building regulations outlawed this type of wood-framed construction in an effort to prevent a repetition of the calamity, but these examples from 1693 revived the earlier tradition. Hare Court, the block of lawyers' chambers on the right, was built in 1894.

Essex Court, Middle Temple, c. 1930. Tranquil gas-lit byways and tree-shaded courts are among the enduring delights of the Temple, but here the scene has changed following the wartime destruction of the late seventeenth-century block of lawyers' chambers on the right. This formerly divided Essex and Brick Courts and was not replaced after the war. Another lost feature is the John Albin's wig and robe shop, centre left.

Clifford's Inn, off Fleet Street, c. 1905. In common with the Temple, Clifford's inn was another community of lawyers and was founded around 1344. It also featured blocks of venerable chambers set beside an historic hall (left) where dining and other community activities took place. Clifford's Inn was dissolved in 1902 and its buildings other than the gatehouse were demolished in 1936.

High Holborn, c. 1898. The half-timbered façade dating from the 1580s is the street frontage of Staple Inn, an Inn of Chancery with an even lengthier history. The first trainee lawyers inhabited Staple Inn around 1415 – the inn provided legal instruction, board and lodging, as did all four Inns of Chancery. The wonderfully preserved frontage has survived the Fire and the Blitz, and the courtyard at the back has been recreated following war damage. The modest shops on the right would be replaced in 1901 by the far grander Staple Inn Building.

Aldersgate Street, c. 1905. Named after a gate in the City wall (demolished 1761), the Aldersgate Street of a century ago was a thoroughfare of small businesses, shops and the odd hotel. The Star Tavern (far right) stood by Maidenhead Court, a tiny byway lost to war damage and the construction from 1968-76 of the Museum of London. The almost total obliteration of this neighbourhood in the Blitz paved the way for the futuristic Barbican, a residential and cultural enclave whose mighty towers dominate the modern Aldersgate Street.

The former churchyard of St Olave, Silver Street from Falcon Square (London Wall), *c*. 1925. Dotted around the City are the site of medieval churches which were lost in the Great Fire and not rebuilt. Their former existence may be recorded by an informative City Corporation plaque or as here, by a small public garden. St Olave's dated from around 1200 and ministered to a quarter where silversmiths plied their trade. The surrounding streets were rebuilt after the Fire and the old burial ground remained in use, eventually forming part of the now defunct Falcon Square. Here, Silver Street, right and Monkwell Street, top left, were mostly occupied by the garment trade. Monkwell Street ran northwards towards Cripplegate and what would become an area of total destruction in the Second World War. Rising from the bomb sites, the 35-acre barbican Estate was conceived in the 1950s, built from the 1960s and completed in 1981 to give the City a spectacular new residential area and a major centre for the arts.

Finsbury Pavement (Moorgate) from London Wall, c. 1905. A gate in the City wall led to Moorfields, a marshy open area bordered by a causeway, the 'pavement' of the street name. Londoners used the ground for outdoor recreation until the 1770s and building development – the gate was removed in 1760. The Globe Tavern, left, is a rare survival in a war-torn area, and beyond it was the Swan & Hoop tavern, reputedly the birthplace in 1795 of poet John Keats.

Finsbury Pavement (Moorgate) by West Street (Finsbury Circus), c. 1896. The typical London commercial terrace on the right has given way to one of the City's most admired inter-war buildings, Britannic House, which was built form 1921-25 and designed by Sir Edward Lutyens for the Anglo-Persian Oil Co. (BP).

Britannic House incorporates an entrance to Moorgate Tube Station and another imposing frontage to Finsbury Circus. The old name 'West Street' has been abolished.

Bishopsgate Street Without, *c.* 1905. This lengthy street begins in the City's financial heartland and runs northwards through the site of the original Roman and medieval City gate (removed 1760) by Wormwood Street. Until 1911 the street name was suffixed 'Within' or 'Without' depending upon which side of the old gate it was located. The view here is of the northernmost part of the street which had remained in a semi-rural state until the late seventeenth century when Huguenot merchants began creating a virtual new suburb of fine town houses beside the City boundary at Spitalfields. In the photograph, old and new building lines (left) show how the Victorians had begun to widen the street while the centre of the view pictures narrow frontages by Brushfield Street where eye-catching glass-fronted towers are now part of Spitalfields' modern regeneration. Also seen is an enduring landmark, Bishopsgate Institute (1894) with its turrets, spires and fine terracotta front behind which is a library and a centre for the study of London's history.

Opposite above: Bishopsgate Street Within (Bishopsgate), *c.* 1905. Wealthy City merchants once lived here, and the last of one of their mansions, Crosby Hall with its zigzag decoration can be seen in the centre of the picture. It was built for Sir John Crosby in the fifteenth century and stood until 1908 when its stone-built hall was dismantled and reassembled as a riverside mansion in Chelsea. It is now one of London's most distinctive private houses. To the left, the National Provincial Bank features abundant rooftop statuary on what is a highly acclaimed example of Victorian banking architecture.

Opposite below: Bishopsgate Street Within near Camomile Street, *c.* 1905. Everyone turns to look as the thundering hooves and clanging bells of a fire escape on a 'shout' scatters the more sedate traffic. Bishopsgate House, right, housed over twenty separate businesses.

Above: Eldon Street, *c.* 1903. The street dates from the early 1800s and is seen here by Wilson Street where the Red Lion pub (1860s) continues to grace the corner. Also still here is neighbouring Eldon House, a block of Edwardian office chambers and the then newly opened St Mary Moorfield Catholic church whose frontage blends well in the commercial street-scape.

Left: Rose Alley, Bishopsgate, *c.* 1905. Although rebuilt and realigned, this obscure passage still exists alongside several others of a similar nature. In these dark shadowy lanes, daylight was elusive and mirrors reflecting the sky were used to supplement the illumination in rooms where dim gaslight was barely sufficient.

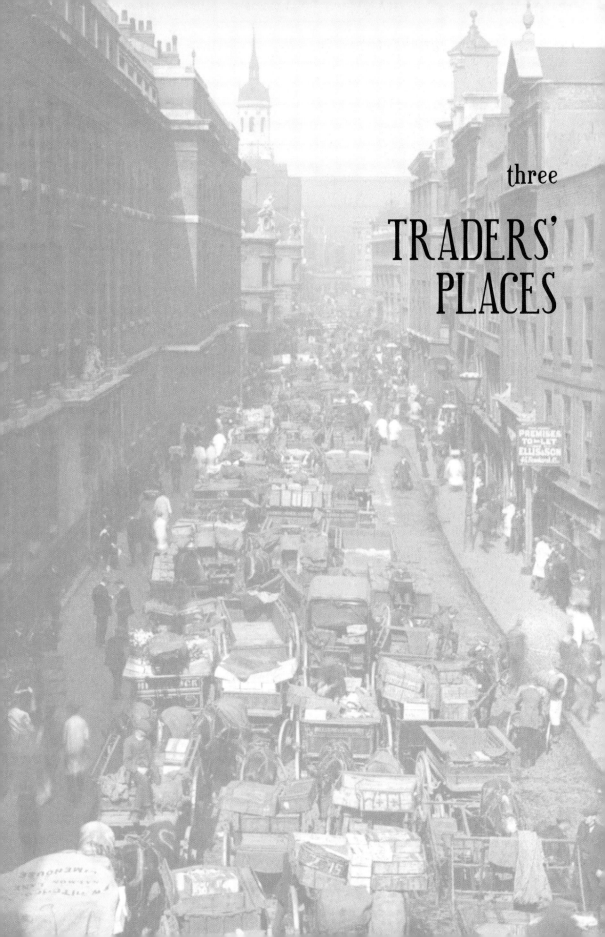

three

TRADERS’ PLACES

Lower Thames Street by Botolph Lane, *c.* 1900. Traders and entrepreneurs have always been drawn to the City and many indeed are the fortunes made (and lost) within the Square Mile. As the world's leading international financial and business centre, the City's glittering towers dominate the scene, but a century ago the Square Mile also accommodated an assortment of craftsmen and small traders who provided services of all kinds from street pitches, markets, workshops and the small shops which once abounded. As land values rose, many old sites and neighbourhoods were lost to grand headquarter buildings and the desirability of a prestigious City address. War devasated swathes of the City and the great rebuilding which came in its wake cost the City even more of its smaller independent business premises. Pubs and refreshment houses catering for the City's daily influx of workers have always prospered and in the Victorian and Edwardian City, George Alexander's cocoa and coffee rooms by Botolph Lane picked up good business from the proximity of Billingsgate Market, as did the modest neighbouring shops. The departure of the fish market in 1982 triggered the demise of more local traders, and grand commercial blocks rule the roost here now.

Above: Hancock, Collis & Co.,
Nos 18-19 Fish Street Hill, near
Billingsgate, *c.* 1905. The proprietors
were paper-bag manufacturers and
waste-paper merchants, but this
multi-faceted business also traded
in household goods and offered a
printing service. With Billingsgate
close by they also sold fish,
'Bloaters and kippers are now in
season' and the shop provided fish
suppers. This odd combination of
trades was successful, and the firm
were here from around 1895 to
1973 before moving away.

Right: Joseph Neil, No. 14
St Dunstan's Hill, Lower Thames
Street, *c.* 1900. Joseph Neil was
a printer and stationer, but it
was the photographic side of his
business which has bequeathed a
fine pictorial legacy of the life and
style of the Billingsgate area at the
beginning of the twentieth century.
An advertisement for 'ball-pointed
pens' uses a term which would
become commonplace in the
1940s with the advent of Mr Biro's
celebrated product.

No. 51 Bartholomew Close, *c.* 1909. Bartholomew Close is a rambling succession of back streets and courts beside the great Priory church of St Bartholomew the Great and St Bartholomew's Hospital. In Edwardian times its venerable if dilapidated buildings housed a large population of small traders including rag and waste merchant Joseph Potter, right, and Samuel Crouch & Sons who provided a range of domestic building services. Today, Bartholomew Close is vibrant with the comings and goings of the hospital whose twentieth-century buildings have gradually replaced the old traders' premises. (Courtesy of the City of London, London Metropolitan Archives)

Above left: No. 90 Bishopsgate by Clark's Place, *c.* 1912. Fred Nix the cigar merchant's aromatic shop took the corner while next door, the Wholesale Watch Co. offered alarm clocks at 1s 11d.

Above right: No. 46 Bishopsgate, *c.* 1912. Bewlay Ltd, the tobacconists (established 1780) had the shop, while a mixture of small firms inhabited the upper floors.

Right: No. 20 Little Britain by Little Montague Court, *c.* 1906. In the City where trading space is at a premium, many modest premises housed a variety of businesses, as here with stationer William Hobbs in the shop and other parts of the building housing an umbrella maker, a patent medicine agent and a cricket-bat maker.

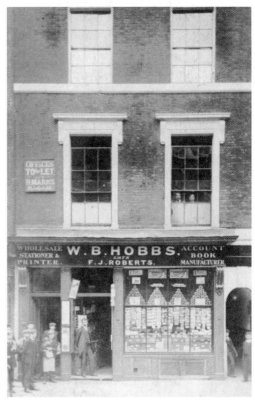

Above: Bambridge Bros., clothing manufacturers, No. 15 Fore Street, *c.* 1909. The firm's representative was Alfred Day who is seen here in his office. Note the antiquated wall-mounted telephone and a copy of that indispensable tool of the modern historian, *Kelly's Post Office London Directory.*

Left: George Adams' Piccadilly Clothiers, Bishopsgate by Camomile Street, *c.* 1912. This was another port-of-call for the well-dressed City gentleman while next door, Shannons, the suppliers of office essentials would have prospered in this highly commercial district.

Mansell, Hunt & Catty Ltd, Ludgate Hill by Ave Maria Lane, *c.* 1935. The firm made Christmas crackers and a wide range of fancy paper ware for the catering trade. This prominent corner spot was taken in the 1970s for the highly controversial Juxon House and in turn by its more acceptable replacement in 2003 as part of the new Paternoster Square.

Thomas Wallis' store from Holborn Circus, *c.* 1906. The City's two largest department stores, Gamages ('The People's Popular Emporium'), and Thomas Wallis' the drapers stood on opposite sides of Holborn before the latter perished in a war-time raid in 1941. This left the Oxford Street branch of the store to carry on the business.

Edwards & Smith Ltd, No. 18 St Alphage Highwalk, London Wall, 1962. After centuries of traditional street life, the futuristic Barbican development introduced the City to a new concept in urban living, the elevated walkway. In a traffic-free environment high above ground level, Barbican's walkways and podia featured shops, pubs and other facilities and linked together the whole labyrinthine complex. In October 1962 the stationery business seen here was the first to occupy retailing space on the new podium. Despite this modernity, a section of the Highwalk south of London Wall has already been abolished.

Middlesex Street (Petticoat Lane Market), c. 1910. Representing a more traditional trading environment, Petticoat lane continues to attract the capital's bargain seekers as it has for the past four centuries. In that time the market has severed diverse communities from the Huguenot settlers of the eighteenth century, the Jewish immigrants of the nineteenth century through to the Asian Londoners of the present day.

Fruit stall, Farringdon Street, *c.* 1905. Costermongers and fruiterers were among a host of street traders whose stalls and barrows once lined the Farringdon Street north of Holborn Viaduct. In its later years, the market became the exclusive preserve of book and print sellers.

Farringdon Market and Smithfield Meat Market, *c.* 1900. Farringdon's wholesale fruit and vegetable market moved here in 1874 from its original site south of Holborn Viaduct. The varied roof line of Smithfield Market (1868) appears further back in a lively street scene.

Central Market, Smithfield Market, Farringdon Street by Snow Hill, *c.* 1904. The ancestry of London's principal meat market can be traced back to the twelfth century when a horse fair was held on the 'smooth field' on the City's edge. The renowned market buildings we know today date from 1868 while the Central Market seen here is from 1879-83. A large sign proclaims 'Corporation Markets for Meat, Poultry, Fish & Provisions', but most of the shops here catered for unrelated trades.

Cornell's Ltd., No. 1 West Smithfield, *c.* 1912. Motor charabancs were an early twentieth century phenomenon and in London were usually employed for outings to sporting events, the seaside and rural beauty spots rather than sightseeing in town. This firm was something of a rarity in the City but has assembled an impressive array of motors for private hire.

Lower Thames Street by Harp Lane, Billingsgate market, *c.* 1905. Powerful fishy aromas and gridlocked market traffic characterised this corner of the City which is seen here in its Edwardian heyday. Fish has been traded here since the eleventh century, but removal of the market to Docklands in 1982 heralded a more sanitised world of shiny office blocks and relentless through traffic. Custom House (1812–17) is on the left with the tower of St Magnus-the-Martyr beyond it.

Above and below: The offices of Guardian Assurance Co., No. 11 Lombard Street, 1914. There are more offices in the City than anywhere else in Britain. These pictures offer an impression of the arrangements in a typical City office some ninety years ago. Here, everything had to be written down by hand and no desk was without its battery of pens, pencils and inkwells. The clerks of the company's foreign department are seen about their daily tasks in the upper picture while chief accountant E.S. Westhorp resides in solitary splendour below. Electronic communication had arrived in the shape of a 'candlestick' telephone, but Mr Westhorp had to make do with an open coal fire for heating.

1 Cheapside from St Paul's Churchyard, *c.* 1890. The muted colours of a Victorian streetscape as preserved by Cheapside photographer George Edward Wood. Among the street's commercial premises is an ancient plane tree which still graces the churchyard of the twelfth-century St Peter Westcheap, a church lost in the Great Fire of 1666.

2 St Paul's Cathedral from the south west, c. 1885. Although colour photography lay decades in the future, this beautifully tinted lantern slide by Messrs Wood of Cheapside gives a fine sense of realism in an age when sepia-tinged monochromes were the order of the day. Here the cathedral rises high above the City's lost landscape of red brick, tile and grey slate, as yet unbroken by the loftier buildings of the modern City. Although the scene had changed little since its great rebuilding following the Fire in 1666, advancing technology was already making a tentative appearance in the shape of a single telegraph pole rising above the rooftops. The first London telephone exchange had opened in Coleman Street in 1879.

3 City landmarks, c. 1896. Continental-style picture postcards were introduced to Britain in 1894, this German-produced example being one of the earlier London ones. Elements of the design reflect the City's maritime heritage.

4 Queenhithe and the Thames waterfront from Southwark Bridge, *c.* 1856. One of the City's earliest tinted photographs depicts the centuries-old quays, warehouses and the sailing ships whose cargoes were landed here. The loftier warehouses of the later Victorian era would soon alter the scene.

5 The City and St Paul's from Southwark, *c.* 1920. This post-war demise of these working City wharves would clear the way for a relocated City of London School (1986), the riverside walkway and the iconic Millennium (Wobbly) Bridge.

Old Temple Bar. 1670-1878.

LONDON, TEMPLE BAR,

Above: 6 Temple Bar, *c.* 1876. The boundary of the Cities of London and Westminster was marked by the last of the City's gates which was removed in 1878 to ease the traffic flow. Temple Bar was reassembled at Theobald's Park, Hertfordshire where it spent over a century in exile before returning to the City in 2004 as part of the new open space at Paternoster Square.

Below: 7 Temple Bar, *c.* 1903. A stone memorial topped by a City dragon was put up here in 1888 to mark the historic entry point into the City. The ancient ceremonies conducted here when the monarch enters the City continued as before.

Above: 8 Fantasy postcard – 'If London Were Venice', Fleet Street, *c.* 1905. Introduced in the 1890s and popularised in the 1900s, picture postcards were a spectalcularly successful medium of communication. Publishers competed for the most interesting and innovative designs among which was a set created from Edwardian photographs which had been retouched to depict London in an unlikely Venetian mode.

Below: 9 Gaslight, Mansion House, *c.* 1920. The greenish glow of gaslighting has illuminated London's streets since 1807 when it was demonstrated in Pall Mall. In post-war years much of the City was still gas-lit, and it can still be seen in the legal enclave of The Temple.

10 Tower Bridge, c. 1895. The Victorians proclaimed the prosperity of the City and its port with this mighty maritime gateway which is seen here in the first year of its working life.

11 College of Arms, Queen Victoria Street, c. 1905. This elegant post-Fire building, home of the royal heralds where armorial matters in this country are regulated, is some 200 years older than the street upon which it stands. The three-sided courtyard seen here was once a quadrangle, but its southern side was removed for the construction of Queen Victoria Street in 1867-71. The College of Arms, part of the Royal Household, received its first charter during the reign of Richard III.

12 Staple Inn, Holborn, *c.* 1885. The sixteenth-century frontage of Staple Inn is a spectacular example of the type of half-timbered architecture commonplace in the City before the Fire, but the style became unfashionable and the buildings 'modernised' with a plaster coating and up-to-date sash windows.

13 Staple Inn and Holborn, *c.* 1928. A late Victorian restoration returned the old frontage to its former glory, its image becoming familiar to generations of smokers through its depiction of 'Old Holborn' tobacco packets. The courtyard at the rear was extensively war-damaged, but it too has been restored.

14 Advertising postcard for Farrow's Bank, *c.* 1910. Postcards like these were an attractive and convenient way of promoting a product or service in the first decades of the twentieth century, this one spreading the word for Farrow's Bank who were based in Cheapside.

15 James Buchanan & Co. Ltd, scotch whisky distillers, No. 26 Holborn, 1903. Buchanan's Black Swan distillery was located behind the company's shop and close to Fetter Lane from where its horse teams were a familiar sight as they set off to deliver the spirit around London. On 1 June 1903, a parade of Buchanan's horse teams made a fine sight as they lined up outside the Holborn shop.

16 The Lord Mayor's Show, 1906. The annual celebration of City life when the incoming Lord Mayor swears his oath of allegiance to the sovereign dates from 1215, and is the most renowned of the City's processions. Seen here is the new Lord Mayor, Sir William Treloar and the Lord Mayor's coach (1757) which is still in use. The picture is from a series of century-old postcards of the event through the ages – this one is 'The Present Day'.

17 Farringdon Market, Farringdon Street, c. 1905. The vegetable market was set up here in 1874 following a move from premises south of Holborn Viaduct. The lively street market also attracted the crowds, and in its final years traded exclusively in the type of material seen here in Ernest Bottom's bookshop; prints, maps and secondhand books

Above left: 18 Ye Olde Cheshire Cheese, off Fleet Street, *c.* 1910. Rebuilt after the Fire, this former chophouse became the haunt of literary giants like Charles Dickens and Dr Johnson of dictionary fame.

Above right: 19 The Royal Mail pub, Noble Street, *c.* 1908. A Victorian pub in a street later stripped of its buildings by the Blitz.

Left: 20 The Golden Axe, St Mary Axe, *c.* 1880. Closure was imminent for this aged hostelry which stood in a street where a fire in the 1890s would destroy many old buildings.

Above left: 21 Shoeblack at Moorgate Street Tube Station, *c.* 1906. It cost 2d for a shoe-shine a century ago.

Above right: 22 Cat's Meat man, *c.* 1906. A traditional London character is seen outside a City branch of 'Ye Mecca', a 'smoking cafe' where chess, draughts and dominoes were on hand for the clients.

Left: 23 Fruit vendor at Moorgate Street Tube Station, *c.* 1906. This familiar figure was usually on hand to tempt the morning commuters as they emerged from the City & South London Railway Station (Northern Line).

Wishing you A Happy Christmas

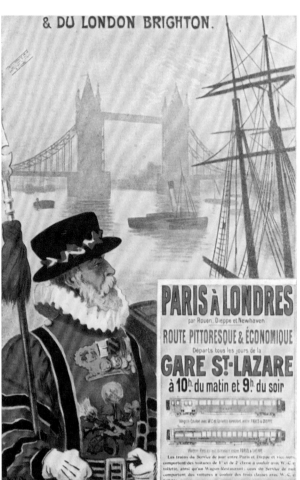

Above: 24 Hansom cab, Salisbury Square, near Fleet Street, *c.* 1906. Joseph Hansom's patent cabs were once as familiar sight as the ubiquitous black cabs of the present day. Nippy and versatile in traffic, the first hansoms appeared around 1834, lasting into the motor age of the twentieth century.

Left: 25 French railway postcard advertisement, *c.* 1910. London's reputation as an international visitor and holiday destination was enhanced in Edwardian times by continental postcards like this which promoted the delights of the City. The Yeoman Warders with their colourful uniforms, as ever epitomised London as did the then new attraction of Tower Bridge. The postcard helpfully included travel information which in those pre-Channel Tunnel days included a short sea voyage.

26 Horse bus, *c.* 1890. A typical omnibus of the Edwardian era which connected North and South London, crossing the City from London Bridge to Liverpool Street in the process.

27 Buses at the Bank of England, *c.* 1924. The colour red was adopted for most London buses following the introduction of route numbers in the Edwardian decade. Before that, buses were colour coded to highlight their routes.

28 Moorgate Street Underground Station, c. 1906. The first part of this complex station opened on 23 December 1865 when it was served by the steam trains of the Metropolitan Railway. They were joined on 25 February 1900 by the electric Tube trains of the City & South London Railway (Northern Line).

29 Bank Tube Station, c. 1906. Bank was the City terminus of the Central London Railway (Central Line) from 1900 – it is seen here with its original wooden platforms. A sign points the way to the interchange with the City & South London Railway which in 1890 was London's first electric Tube.

Above: 30 St Mary the Virgin, Aldermanbury, *c.* 1908. Of possible late Saxon origin, the church was rebuilt by Wren after the Fire, but the Blitz ended its life in the City. The church's masonry was later salvaged and from 1965-69 the building was re-erected at Westminster College, Fulton, Missouri in honour of Sir Winston Churchill. A City garden marks the old site.

Right: 31 St Ethelburga's church, Bishopsgate Street, *c.* 1908. This tiniest of medieval churches hides behind E.H. Robinson's spectacle shop while its ancient stonework lies behind a coat of rendering. The church survived the Fire and the Blitz but not a terrorist's bomb in 1993. Rebuilding has since restored this much-loved landmark.

32 St Paul's Cathedral from Cannon Street, *c.* 1948. The cathedral stood defiant in the face of the bombing raids of the Second World War but its surrounding neighbourhoods fared less well. To the right the church of St Augustine with St Faith lies burnt out amid the ruins of Watling Street and Old Change. The low brick walls surrounding bomb sites were a familiar sight in the post-war City.

33 St Mary-le-Bow, Cheapside and war ruins from Old Change, *c.* 1948. Wren's great tower looks out over a nightmare landscape in which almost every building between St Paul's and St Mary's was destroyed. The church would be restored from 1956-64.

The Blickensderfer Co. Nos 9-10 Cheapside, *c.* 1905. Strident advertising for the range of office equipment offered by this firm of typewriter specialists. Also on offer were 'computing machines' which at this early date were electro-mechanical tabulators – electric computers did not appear commercially until the 1950s.

Construction site, Gracechurch Street, 1913. The City is constantly evolving and no one is usually far from a building site. In the early twentieth century, new constructions still followed the low-rise Victorian tradition, as here where new premises for the Mercantile Bank of India and the Hong Kong & Shanghai Bank take shape behind a dense cocoon of old-fashioned wooden scaffolding.

Above: Outside the Stock Exchange, Threadneedle Street, *c.* 1906. The first Stock Exchange was at premises in Sweeting's Alley which were acquired by a group of brokers in 1773 – a move to the first purpose-built exchange in Capel Court followed in 1802. A new building in Threadneedle Street opened in 1854 – this was replaced by a mighty tower which opened in 1972 while another move in 2004 brought the Stock Exchange to the new Paternoster Square.

Left: The Baltic Exchange, St Mary Axe, *c.* 1903. The Baltic Exchange which handled maritime business originated in 1744 at a coffee house in Threadneedle Street, and after several moves, built the renowned Exchange which is seen here soon after completion. A terrorist outrage wrecked the building in 1992 and subsequent demolition cleared the way for the most iconic of the City's new wave of commercial buildings, the Swiss Re Tower, whose unusual shape invoked Londoner's affectionate name for it, 'The Gherkin'.

The Coal Exchange, Lower Thames Street by St Mary-at-Hill, Billingsgate, *c.* 1912. Although the city possesses a wealth of fine and historic buildings, it has through fire, war and redevelopment, lost many others which would be treasured today. A cruel loss occurred in 1962 with the demolition for road widening of the Coal Exchange, a rare early iron-framed building dating from 1849. It featured a glass-domed rotunda around which office space for coal dealers was elegantly arranged. The building's demise speeded the traffic but with it went the final link with Billingsgate's lesser-known role as a coal wharf.

The Old Bell Inn, Holborn, *c.* 1890. Venerable coaching inns featuring wooden galleries around a central courtyard were once commonplace in central London, but with the rise of railway travel and decline in coaching their numbers dwindled away. The Bell was the last of these inns to survive in the City – it was rebuilt as a pub in 1897.

Ye Old Cheshire Cheese, Wine Office Court, Fleet Street, *c.* 1938. Although the number of pubs in the City has declined with a falling population, it still contains many mellow hostelries which are cherished by the City folk who crowd them at lunchtimes and after work. Some of these establishments have been here for centuries, notably the old writers' and journalists' pub, Ye Olde Cheshire Cheese. It originated in the 1500s and was rebuilt in 1667 following the Fire. The Cheese boasts an illustrious former clientele including Dr Johnson, Dickens and Thackeray.

The London Stone, Cannon Street by Salters Hall Court, *c.* 1920. The pub was named after the mysterious London Stone, a carved limestone block known to have existed around 1100 and which was displayed behind an iron grille set into a wall of St Swithin's church, right. This Wren church was a wartime casualty, but from 1960 the stone had a new home on a Cannon Street office block where it can still be seen. The pub now occupies the neighbouring building, left.

At the Bull and Bell, Ropemaker Street, *c.* 1933. A popular pub will often seek to offer its clientele something to distinguish it from its fellows, as here where landlord Walter Hallpike took to rearing crocodiles on the premises. It is tempting to wonder whether the beasts had a role to play by hurrying along recalcitrant drinkers at closing time!

The Tiger Tavern, Tower Hill, *c.* 1925. This venerable hostelry stood on Tower Hill from around 1500 and retained the mummified remains of a cat reputed to have been stroked by Queen Elizabeth I. Rebuilt many times, the tavern is seen here following a reconstruction in 1913. The Tiger's final incarnation came in 1965 as part of a particularly forbidding office block, but when that was mercifully demolished the Tiger, sadly went with it.

The Three Kingdoms Tavern, Lower Thames Street, Billingsgate, *c.* 1903. This image by local photographer Joseph Neil shows one of the small but busy pubs which were everywhere in old Billingsgate where hard work in the fish market generated healthy thirsts. Note the road surfacing of granite setts – these were essential to withstand the constant onslaught of heavy market traffic.

Above: George Thorne, wine merchants, Crutched Friars, *c.* 1910. The area around Crutched Friars was noted for its abundance of bonded warehouses containing some of the considerable quantities of wines and spirits imported through the Port of London. Here is the entrance to the cellars of a local wine merchant.

Right: E.E. Foster & Co., wine merchant, 1a Gutter Lane, Cheapside, *c.* 1909. This was the Edwardian face of a profession which has served London since Roman times. The Worshipful Company of Vintners, one of the City's medieval Livery Companies represented the interests of the City's wine importers since the fourteenth century – the company's hall has an imposing presence by the river off Upper Thames Street.

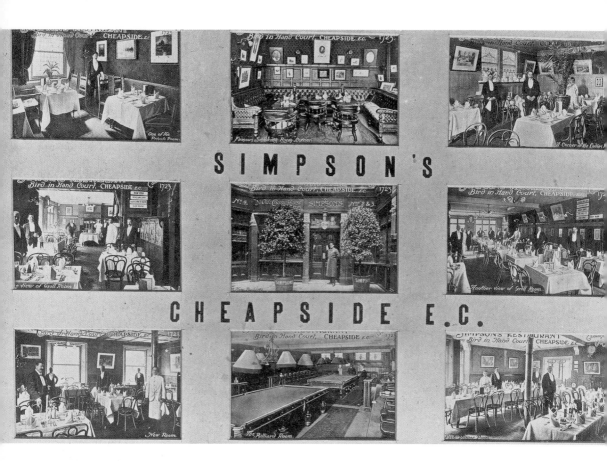

Above: Simpson's Restaurant, Bird-in-Hand Court, Cheapside, *c.* 1910. This most traditional of City restaurants evolved around 1723 at the Three Tuns Tavern in Bell Alley, Billingsgate and naturally for that area, the menu specialised in fish from the local market. A move to the former premises of the Queen's Arms pub in Bird-in-Hand Court followed, and in 1898 a new Simpson's arose after a fire. Simpson's was one of the last City restaurants where grace was said before a meal, and in another tradition, anyone who correctly guessed the weight of the cheese displayed in one of the dining rooms was rewarded with champagne.

Left: A German restaurant, No. 154 Cheapside, *c.* 1908. In the years leading up to the First World War, London was home to a sizeable German population and a wide variety of German-owned businesses including restaurants. These were popular with Londoners who enjoyed the continental cuisine and with German exiles nostalgic for a taste of their homeland.

Above: Black & White Milk Bar, No. 68 Fleet Street, 1930s. Trends in popular catering come and go, and in the 1930s there was a new phenomenon, the milk bar. The Black & White chain of smart, bright bars quickly established itself alongside a campaign promoting the health-giving properties of the drink – this Fleet Street branch was the first of the new breed.

Right: J. Lyons & Co. Ltd, No. 61 King William Street, *c.* 1910. From his first shop in Piccadilly in 1894, caterer Joseph Lyons rapidly established a network of Lyons' Corner Houses and Tea Shops which in their time were as familiar as sight as the great catering chains of the present day. The shop seen here was one of a pair in this street and lasted from 1903 to 1920 – a Ladies' room and a Smoking Room were among the amenities.

Above: Shoe black by the Royal Exchange, *c.* 1906. This was a useful trade a century ago when London's large horse population added its own hazards underfoot. Shoe blacks tended to congregate in busy public places like railway stations or as here, the forecourt of the Royal Exchange where there was a constant stream of City workers anxious to arrive at the office clean shod.

Below: Pavement artist, *c.* 1906. The street was the workplace for these popular characters who could be found wherever visitors could be relied upon to contribute to the traditional hat. The paving stones of Tower Hill were the canvas for this gentleman.

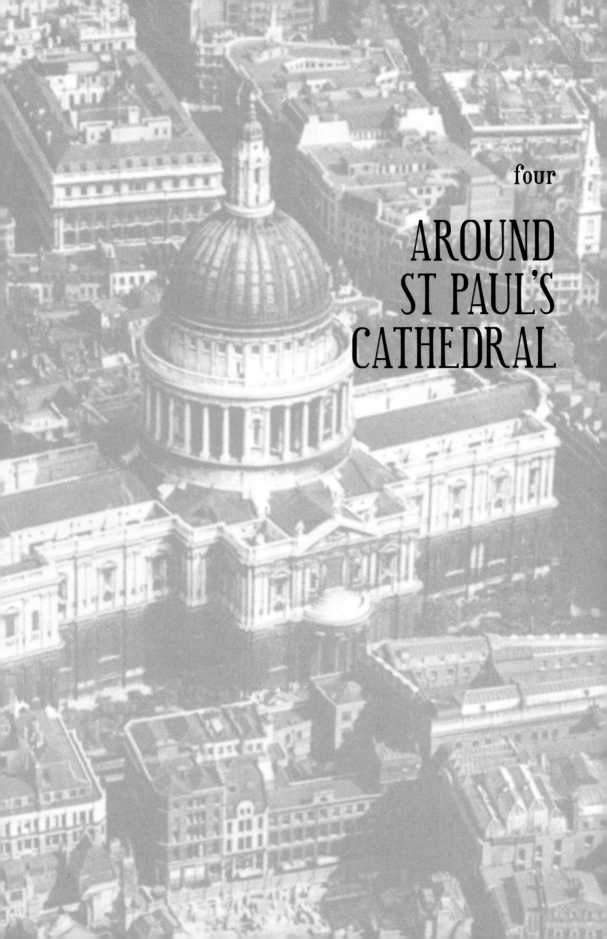

four

AROUND ST PAUL'S CATHEDRAL

St Paul's Cathedral, *c.* 1870. There has been a place of worship on the hilltop site the Romans once used as a vantage point since 604 AD when the first St Paul's was built. By 1310 St Paul's was a vast Gothic masterpiece towering high above the City, its lofty spire given added prominence by the cathedral's elevated site. In 1666 and with the spire already felled by lightning, the cathedral perished in the Great Fire, but St Paul's rose again, this time with a startling design by Wren which was unlike anything Londoners had seen before. The Victorian photograph shows St Paul's as Wren may have seen it, riding high above a sea of tile and slate roofs belonging to the ancient neighbourhoods which had themselves been rebuilt after the Fire but to the medieval street pattern. The Blitz of 1941 left the City in ruins around its cathedral which miraculously survived, but which destroyed the old wholesale booksellers' quarter of Paternoster Row to the north. Post-war rebuilding brought the visually and historically destructive Paternoster Square scheme which, after a mercifully short life was replaced by a new Paternoster whose design is more appropriate to the precincts of a world-renowned cathedral.

Ludgate Street (Ludgate Hill) 1880s. With its origins as a Roman highway, the street boasts an even lengthier history than the cathedral which looks down upon it. As the name suggests, Ludgate was once a route through the City wall, and the street was lined with the wooden houses of medieval London until all was lost in the Great Fire. Despite a new cathedral crowning the hilltop, the rebuilt Ludgate Street retained its narrowness with the great west front of St Paul's theatrically revealing itself with every step with which it was approached. This Victorian picture catches the street during its widening programme from 1863–91 which opened up a broader view of the cathedral – the contrast between the old and new building lines is easily seen by Creed Lane, right. The building of Juxon House in the 1970s once more obtruded into this famous cityscape until a twenty-first century replacement gave the cathedral a more agreeable setting.

St Paul's Cathedral and St Paul's Churchyard from Cheapside, *c.* 1870. The cathedral is an awesome presence in the City of the present day, but in mid-Victorian times when the streets were still filled with the small-scale buildings of the post-Fire era, St Paul's overshadowed everything in dramatic style. Seen here on the right by Paternoster Row are the modest premises of City drapers, Nicholson's, who set up in 1843 and rebuilt in grander style in 1900. Paternoster Row was a narrow street where rosary sellers once plied their trade, as did lacemakers and silkmen in the seventeenth century when it was a resort of the fashionable, including City diarist Samuel Pepys and his family. The premises of latter-day laceman George Nock can be seen on the Cheapside corner, left.

Opposite above: St Paul's Churchyard and Paternoster Row from Cheapside, *c.* 1901. This is the popular Nicholson's department store shortly after its newly rebuilt premises had opened. Trading continued here until 1965 after which the dreary Paternoster precinct replaced all but one of the buildings which had survived the war.

Below: St Paul's Churchyard, *c.* 1905. Old St Paul's Churchyard was a centre of the book and printing trades and notoriously, a place of public execution – those concerned in the Gunpowder Plot of 1605 were duly dispatched here. A fashionable shopping area developed in the wake of the cathedral's post-Fire rebuilding and an element of that remained in Edwardian times.

Paternoster Square. The first Paternoster
Square was created on the cleared site
of Newgate Market, a grim place where
animals were slaughtered for the meat trade.
The market's activities were transferred to
Smithfield in 1869 following which the
site was built up with shops, warehouses
and refreshment houses which lasted until
wartime bombs virtually obliterated the area.
The closely-packed buildings were typical of
the Victorian City (*top*) photographs, *c.* 1930
as were Joseph Dolphin's dining rooms, seen
around 1910, (*bottom left*).

Above and below: Pre-war and post-war comparison views around St Paul's; *c.*1930 (*above*), *c.* 1950 (*below*). The Second World War spared the cathedral but devastated its surroundings, as is seen in the lower picture which shows the bomb sites following the clearance of unstable ruins. The old street pattern can still be seen, however, with Paternoster Square, left, and the now lost Ivy Lane running up to Newgate Street to the left of it. St Paul's Churchyard is seen with most of its buildings still standing, albeit damaged. The destruction would be completed for the building of the grim Paternoster scheme which would disfigure the area for over three decades until a more humane plan would restore some lost dignity.

Building Paternoster Square, 1960s. The problem of rebuilding London after the Blitz was being addressed as early as 1942, but with ongoing hostilities and long years of post-war austerity, it would be two decades before rebuilding on the area of devastation to the north of St Paul's could begin. The fine site in the shadow of one of the world's great cathedrals presented an opportunity to enhance its setting with exciting but respectful architecture, but what finally arose was a dreary collection of dull office blocks, shops and a raised concrete piazza. At first the scheme was perceived as bright and modern and the new piazza allowed views of the north side of St Paul's which had for centuries been obscured by the densely built neighbourhoods behind St Paul's Churchyard. As it is seen here, the piazza was utilised for public events, but its elevated layout lessened the cathedral's presence, and partly obscured Wren's restored Chapter House, left, the only building to survive the developer's onslaught. As the years passed, the Paternoster scheme soon became outmoded and was derided by Londoners as being grossly inappropriate for its revered location, and demolition was the inevitable outcome. This opened the way for a new Paternoster Square which then provided modestly scaled architecture (including a new Stock Exchange) set around an attractive, lively public space. There was also a revival of some of the narrow vistas of the cathedral's dome seen between the buildings, and the old City gate, Temple Bar, duly restored and resited, creating a major new visitor attraction.

Watling Street by Friday Street, *c.* 1920. Formerly a principal street in the City with five churches along its length, Watling Street can claim an 800-year history along with enviable views of St Paul's Cathedral. The Blitz destroyed the western end of the street seen here, but the eastern end by Bow Lane (behind the camera) retains the narrow roadway and small commercial buildings so characteristic of the old City.

Old Change, *c.* 1912. Old Change formerly ran to the east of St Paul's linking Cheapside with Cannon Street and containing until 1884, the premises of St Paul's School. Known to date before 1293, Old Change's narrowness hints at its antiquity and its name at its derivation from the King's Exchange which stood here. This was a place at which silver and gold bullion could be exchanged for the coinage of the day – the street was called 'Old' Change when this facility moved away.

Although Old Change was destroyed in the Blitz, one element of the street remains, albeit in a new setting. This is the tower of the church of St Augustine-with-St Faith, Watling Street, a Wren rebuilding of a church dating from around 1148. Although the church was lost, the restored tower now forms part of the complex of buildings put up from 1962-67 for St Paul's Cathedral Choir School. Old Change no longer exists as a street, but its former course can be traced as a footpath through Festival Garden, an open space created out of old bomb sites in 1951, the year of the Festival of Britain. Today, a fine new street called New Change runs close by and takes the modern traffic while partly preserving the ancient name (City of London, London Metropolitan Archives)

Right: St Paul's from Cannon Street, *c.* 1938. One of the most popular of the modern views of St Paul's is that from Cannon Street, but in pre-war years the scene was very different with Victorian warehouses crowding in upon the cathedral. The traveller towards St Paul's was, however, rewarded with this dramatic revelation of the dome as the buildings opened out by St Paul's Churchyard. Through the benevolence of the Gardeners' Company, the old bomb sites here were transformed into a colourful City garden.

Below: War ruins off Cannon Street, *c.* 1949. Clearance of war-damaged buildings opened out enticing vistas of familiar landmarks and although rebuilding gave some of the views a fleeting existence, others like the grand panorama from Cannon Street were too precious to lose.

The view here is of a rubble-strewn wasteland in which Friday Street and Bread Street have been shorn of their buildings and St Augustine's church stands ruined by Watling Street. Post-war reconstruction would bring new commercial blocks around Watling Street and New Change while the gardens at Cannon Street would preserve the open aspect.

ST. PAUL'S CATHEDRAL AMONG THE BOMBED RUINS.

The south–west tower of St Paul's from Godliman Street, *c.* 1930. Until 1890 this section of Godliman Street was called Paul's Chain, a name thought to have been derived from the chain put across old St Paul's Churchyard during cathedral services. The old properties to the left have long gone as has the tiny entry to Paul's Bakehouse Court, the historic location of the cathedral's bakery.

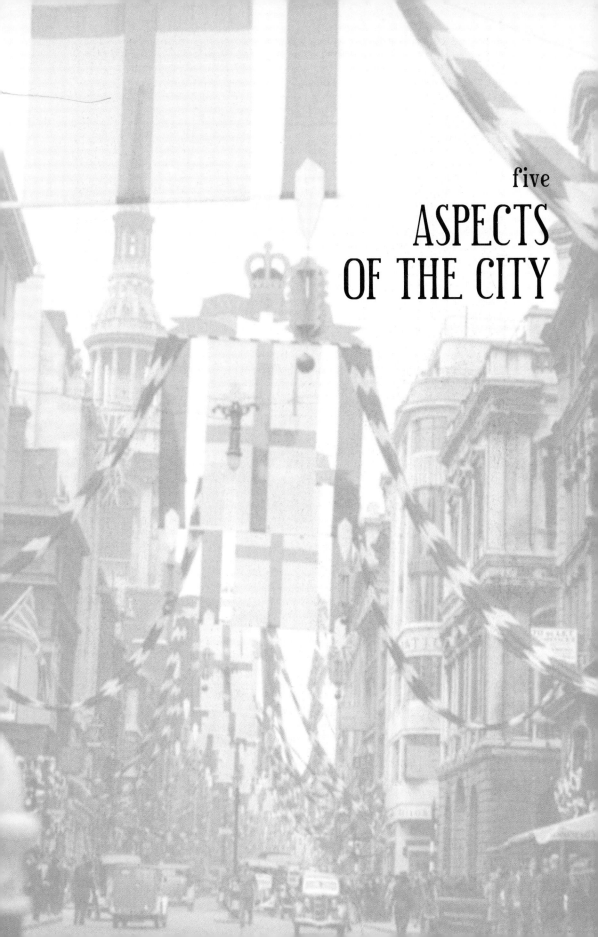

five

ASPECTS
OF THE CITY

Queen Victoria's Diamond Jubilee, 22 June 1897. London provides a focus for the nation at times of celebration with its inspirational displays of patriotism and pageantry. Jubilee Day, 1897 provided spectacular military and royal processions and a Service of Thanksgiving at St Paul's Cathedral. There was a rehearsal for the event on the preceding day, and despite the absence of the Queen, seats in the special viewing stands changed hands for 30 guineas a time. In that age of opulent millinery, ladies were politely requested to wear hats and bonnets with 'limited trimmings'. On Jubilee Day itself the service featured mass choirs and bands with around 800 musicians gathered on the cathedral steps. Due to her frailty, the Queen was obliged to remain in her carriage for the service which is seen here in part including the carriages of visiting royalty.

Queen Victoria at London Bridge, 22 June 1897. The Queen's Jubilee procession took the traditional Royal route from Westminster, entering the City of London at Temple Bar and reaching St Paul's via Fleet Street and Ludgate Hill. The return journey crossed into Southwark at London Bridge before recrossing the Thames at Westminster Bridge. The lavishly embellished London Bridge was a popular viewpoint with spectators clinging to every available space, while on the river a flotilla of steamers and tugs sounded a Royal salute with their steam whistles as the Queen's carriage crossed the Thames. As dusk fell, the streets and buildings were beautified with a few of the new style electric displays supplementing the traditional gas and oil lamps and displays of fairy lights. There was also a grand firework display to mark the historic day.

Silver Jubilee decorations, Cheapside, May 1935. The first Royal Jubilee of the twentieth century was marked by traditional processions and a Service of Thanksgiving at St Paul's Cathedral which was attended by a congregation of distinguished guests from around the world. Colourful flags and bunting once more adorned the capital, notably in Fleet Street, Ludgate Hill and in Cheapside where the ancient church of St Mary-le-Bow had all but disappeared behind the patriotic displays. The view here is rather poignant as no one present in Cheapside at this joyful time could have predicted that within a few years the street would lay devastated by war damage.

Opposite above: Coronation decorations, the Royal Exchange and Bank of England, August 1902. Lasting sixty-three years, such was the longevity of Queen Victoria's reign, most Britons had known no other monarch and had never lived through a Coronation. With the new century, however, there was soon a new sovereign, and on 9 August 1902 King Edward VII with Queen Alexandra were crowned in Westminster Abbey thus beginning the peaceful and prosperous Edwardian era.

Opposite below: Coronation decorations, Ludgate Circus, June 1911. The Edwardian decade passed all too quickly, and on 22 June 1911 King George V and Queen Mary's Coronation celebrations filled the nation's streets with vivid displays of patriotism. As ever, the City rose to the occasion with ceremonial arches at Temple Bar and London Bridge and decorated streets of which this was a typical example.

Above: Queen Victoria Street, Silver Jubilee Day, 6 May 1935; 9.15 a.m. It is Jubilee Day and an amateur photographer's snapshot (first in a sequence of four) captures something of that particular mood of the City as it prepares for one of its great days. Crowds are beginning to line the streets in the early sunshine to join those who have camped out overnight to get the best view.

Left: A Pearly King at Ludgate Hill, Jubilee Day, 1935. The entrepreneurial spirit of the City is in evidence here as one of London's cockney Pearly Kings offers souvenirs of a memorable day. 'Pearlies' were originally costermongers, and with their association (founded 1911) devote themselves to charitable work.

Above: Victoria Embankment, near The Temple, Jubilee Day, 1935. Hours spent waiting to see Royal processions can be notoriously hard on the feet, but having enjoyed the pageantry, six young ladies, still in their Jubilee hats, find the Thames waters a blessed relief. Meanwhile, a family picnics and a City man takes refuge in his newspaper.

Right: Aftermath of the Jubilee, Fleet Street. As the crowds make their way home, the City slowly returns to normal and a mountain of litter awaits the City's cleansing department. In the distance, a colourful display still disguises the Ludgate Hill railway bridge, but closer to the camera, the excitement had proved too much for one motor car which has expired in the midst of the post-Jubilee debris.

Above: Coronation Eve, 1 June 1953. Queen Elizabeth II acceded to the throne upon the death of her father, George VI, on 6 February 1952 – the Coronation took place on a rainy 2 June 1953. This is the scene to the east of St Paul's Cathedral where the ravages of war are still evident – the building on the left being the only one hereabouts to remain in a habitable condition. The burnt out St Augustine's, Watling Street is seen with St Mary-le-Bow to the right of it. The colourful standards of City Livery Companies are flying above Festival Garden which was created by one of them, the Worshipful Company of Gardeners.

Left: Coronation decorations near Guildhall, June 1953. A good display of flags and bunting adds colour to a City still drab with post-war austerity and bomb sites.

The Lord Mayor of London, Sir William Treloar and Lady Treloar, Mansion House, June 1907. The Queen's Fete was a glittering three-day fund-raising event held at Mansion House on behalf of London's crippled children. The fete was opened by Queen Alexandra on 13 June and among those who presided over stalls selling fancy goods were no less than four princesses, while other notables included Louis Wain who entertained visitors with his drawings of comic cats. The Lord Mayor and Lady Mayoress are seen seated in a Hills-Martine motor car which was later wheeled into the Egyptian Hall and auctioned in aid of the cripples' fund. Sir William founded a home for crippled children at Alton, Hampshire with part of the funds raised at the fete.

Beating the bounds, All Hallows, Barking-by-the-Tower, Ascension Day, 1933. Ancient traditions and ceremonies are an important part of City life, as here where the parish boundaries of a church whose history began before 1086 are being marked by beating with willow wands.

LONDON. St. Ethelburgha, Bishopsgate Street. No. 1809.

St Ethelburga, Bishopsgate Street Within, *c.* 1920. Among the elements which distinguish the City from other parts of London is the priceless legacy of its churches. The Square Mile once contained around 100 of them, the majority dating from medieval times and serving tiny but populous parishes in the old residential City. Fire, war and a declining population gradually eroded their numbers to around forty in the present day. The photograph of 1920s Bishopsgate catches the diminutive and almost hidden St Ethelburga's church whose records date from around 1250. Modernists had at some point rendered over the church's aged ragstone masonry, but in 1932 that covering would be stripped away along with Edward Robinson's optician's shop which stood guard on either side of the church entrance – the congregation had been obliged to pass through the shop to enter the church. The neighbouring buildings would soon be replaced by grander ones but the church would survive the war only to be felled in a terrorist outrage in 1993. St Ethelburga's was recreated in 2002 using as much original material as possible and it now flourishes as a Centre for Reconciliation and Peace, while behind it rises the City's iconic 'Gherkin' offering one of the great contrasts between ancient and modern for which the Square Mile is famed.

Opposite above: Great St Helen's, Bishopsgate, *c.* 1920. The trees mask another remarkable medieval survival, St Helen's church which lay beyond the reach of the Fire and was also spared by the Blitz. The church is a glorious amalgamation of the remains of a Benedictine nunnery founded around 1210 and an even older parish church. The parallel naves of both churches reveal the alterations of succeeding centuries and there is a treasury of monuments to the City folk who worshipped and are buried here.

Opposite below: By the south door, St Helen's Bishopsgate, *c.* 1920. A street musician entertains against a backdrop of the church's age-blackened walls, part of which has since been obscured by the building of new church offices. The door is dated 1633.

LONDON — Great St. Helen's, Bishopsgate. No. 186?

ST. MARY-AT-HILL.

Above: St Mary-at-Hill, *c.* 1906. The classic beauty of a Wren church interior with its rich dark woodwork and white columns and pilasters. The church survived the war, but in 1988 a fire caused serious damage to the roof and woodwork. In Edwardian times, the organ's contribution to the church music was supplemented by the technology of the day, a horn gramophone, right.

Left: St Mary-at-Hill and St Margaret Pattens, *c.* 1925. The church and the street have the same name – the church of St Mary-at-Hill being spotted in the picture by its prominent clock. Beyond it and across Eastcheap is St Margaret Pattens, Rood Lane, a twelfth-century church rebuilt by Wren from 1684-87.

St Mildred church, Bread Street from Huggin Lane (Huggin Hill) *c.* 1930. First-century Romans created a baths complex on these sunny south-facing slopes overlooking the river, but by the thirteenth century it was Hoggene Lane, a place where livestock was kept. The thirteenth-century St Mildred's church overlooked the lane, but having succumbed to the Fire it was rebuilt from 1681 by Wren only for it to be damaged, terminally this time in the Blitz. To the right is the built-over site of another Wren church, St Michael Queenhithe (demolished 1876), but railings still fronted the disused graveyard. Everything seen here has now gone, but at the top of the hill a garden commemorates Frederick Cleary (1905-84), a member of the City's Court of Common Council and Chairman of the Metropolitan Public Gardens Association – Mr Cleary constantly campaigned for more open space in the city.

College Hill and the church of St Michael, Paternoster Royal, *c.* 1920. College Hill is a narrow byway rich in associations with Sir Richard (Dick) Whittington, a prosperous mercer and three times Lord Mayor of London. Sir Richard was buried in the church whose records date from around 1100 – he also funded the rebuilding of the church in 1409 and an adjoining college of priests. The church was rebuilt by Wren (1694) and a 'blue plaque' today marks the site of Dick Whittington's house, left.

Laurence Pountney Hill, *c.* 1906. The sites of the City's lost churches are scattered about the Square Mile, sometimes with a plaque to mark their former existence or as here, with a garden created out of an old churchyard. The church of St Laurence Pountney dated from the thirteenth century but was not rebuilt after the Fire. The scene here with its post-Fire houses in the background remains virtually unchanged in a century.

Above: St Sepulchre-without-Newgate, Holborn Viaduct, *c.* 1920. This, the largest of the City parish churches, was of twelfth-century origin, rebuilt in the fifteenth century and restored from 1667-71. There were links with Newgate Gaol which stood opposite and the church still has a handbell which was rung on the night before an execution – a single bell in the tower was one of the last sounds heard by a condemned prisoner.

Right: St Mary Somerset, Upper Thames Street by Fye Foot Lane, 1956. First recorded around 1150 and later rebuilt by Wren, this small church lost everything except its tower in 1869. This survives to the present day together with a small garden – the tower's setting in 1956 was quite peaceful with small commercial premises and bomb sites all around. Fye Foot Lane was once called Five Foot Lane due to its narrowness – it exists today as a bridge over the thunderous traffic of Upper Thames Street.

St Bartholomew's Hospital and the church of St Bartholomew the Less, West Smithfield, *c.* 1865. Notable among the treasures of the City are the church of St Bartholomew the Great and the adjoining hospital, both of which were founded in 1123 by Rahere, a courtier of King Henry I. The little church of St Bartholomew the Less was recorded in 1184 when it served as a hospital chapel before it attained a unique role as the church of a parish entirely confined to the precincts of the hospital. 'Barts' has continually modernised with the passing centuries but the church retains the fifteenth-century tower seen here.

The Gatehouse, St Bartholomew the Great, *c.* 1925. The church, originally an Augustinian priory, lies behind the half-timbered gatehouse (1598) which tops a thirteenth-century arch through which worshippers once passed directly into the priory's south aisle from the street. Long plastered over, the gatehouse's timbers were revealed following First World War damage.

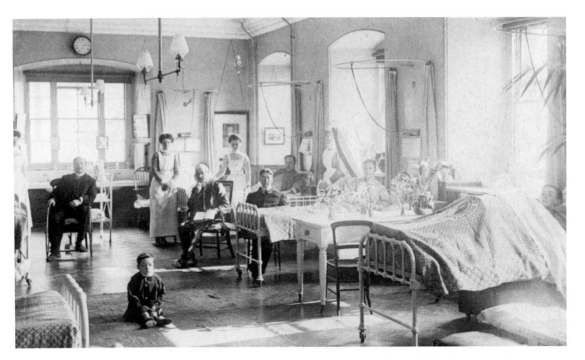

Darker Ward, St Bartholomew's Hospital, *c.* 1905. After nearly 900 years of devoted health care, 'Barts' retains a special place in the hearts of most Londoners. This Edwardian ward was bright with pot plants and the hospital's distinctive bed coverings.

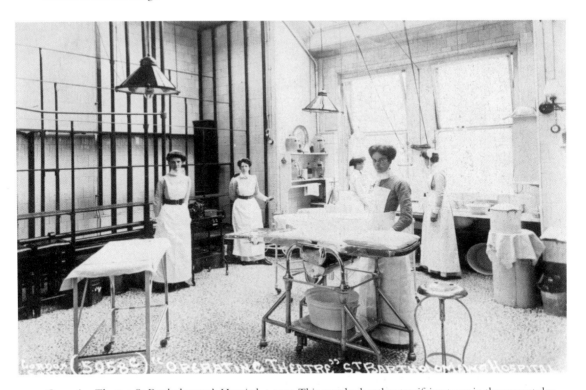

Operating Theatre, St Bartholomew's Hospital, *c.* 1905. This may look rather terrifying to us in the present day, but a century ago these facilities were the last word in modernity complete with the latest electric lighting to assist the surgeons. As ever, the nurses were immaculately turned out in their full-length uniforms.

Left: First World War damage, Bartholomew Close. It is 1915, a time when this country had become unused to fighting its wars on home soil. It was also the dawn of a new age of aerial conflict with Zeppelin airships capable of delivering death and destruction into the capital itself. On 8 September 1915 Zeppelin L13 commanded by Kapitan Leutnant Heinrich Mathy mounted one of the earliest bombing raids on London – this included the incident seen here when two people perished in Bartholomew Close. There was much damage to the Bartholomew diary and adjoining textile warehouse but mercifully, the hospital was spared.

Below: National Restaurant, New Bridge Street, July 1918. At a time of wartime emergency, the Ministry of Food's National Kitchens set up a series of communal restaurants to provide cheap and sustaining meals. The popularity of this one in former premises of Messrs Spiers & Pond's department store is all too evident.

NATIONAL RESTAURANT, NEW BRIDGE STREET, JULY, 1918.

Photographed from the Premises
of L. & R. Wooderson.

Reading the Proclamation of Pea
at the Old Cheapside Cross, Woo
June 30th 1919.

Peace Proclamation, Cheapside by Wood Street, 1919. Following the signing of the Treaty of Versailles which ended the First World War, the Royal Proclamation of Peace was publicly read at five places in London, three of which were in the City. On 30 June 1919, the colourful heraldic procession entered the City at Temple Bar and the Proclamation was read at a ceremony near Chancery Lane. With its escort of Life Guards the procession moved on to Cheapside where Windsor Herald Mr W.A. Lindsay once more delivered the Proclamation, at the end of which and to the joyful sound of trumpets, the procession moved off to the Royal Exchange for the final reading. As ever, the ceremonials attracted large crowds despite the showery weather, and in Cheapside office windows gave a grand view of the proceedings. At the premises of the London Glove Co., two intrepid observers had climbed outside for a closer look, centre.

The place chosen for the Cheapside ceremony was an historic one for it was the site of the Chepe Cross, the Eleanor Cross which stood here in the City's western market from 1290-1643. The peace celebrated on this day proved to be short lived and in a mere two decades this country was once again at war, and by the end of it, Cheapside and many other streets in London lay in ruins.

London Wall and St Giles Cripplegate, *c*. 1942. The Second World War changed the face of the City more completely than any event since the Great Fire, with some areas totally destroyed, as here. In the background, the twelfth-century church where Shakespeare worshipped and Oliver Cromwell married lies burnt out in a wasteland which would in time be reborn as the Barbican Estate.

St Paul's from Distaff Lane, *c*. 1942. Symbolising the spirit of the nation at a time of war, St Paul's remains an imposing sight amid the ruins of its surrounding streets.

Bomb sites between Mark Lane, Mincing Lane and Fenchurch Street, *c.* 1945. This is another area of the City where some streets lost nearly all their buildings including Mincing Lane where the hall of the Clothworkers' Company has stood, albeit frequently rebuilt, since the fifteenth century – a post-war rebuilding would follow from 1955-58. To the right is the tower of All Hallows Staining, a pre-Fire relic which the Clothworkers' Company preserved when the greater part of the church was pulled down in 1870.

Newgate Street after an air-raid, 1941. The dome of the Central Criminal Court, Old Bailey, is seen at the end of a rubble-strewn Newgate Street during the Blitz.

Queen Victoria Street by Peter's Hill, *c.* 1945. Disaster upon disaster as a steam-driven traction engine which was being used to clear heavy debris from a bomb site crashes through an unstable floor into a former basement. Peter's Hill in the background is now part of the scenic walkway linking the Millennium Bridge with St Paul's Cathedral.

Ludgate Gardens, *c.* 1948. After the war, bomb sites across the City were put to a variety of uses, as here where a mini-garden centre beautifies a derelict site off Ludgate Hill. Umbrella makers James Ince & Son of Bishopsgate were among the firms promoting their garden products here. Holborn Viaduct Station is seen on the left, while to the right, the Old Bailey rises above lingering war ruins.

Above: Crowds at the Central Criminal Courts, Old Bailey, *c.* 1910. The opening of the Central Criminal Courts by King Edward VII and Queen Alexandra on 27 February 1907 brought a rather lighter touch to a site which had been occupied by the grim Newgate Prison, the last manifestation of which dated from 1778 – the prison itself had been here since the twelfth century. The picture may have been taken during a high-profile trial, possibly that of Dr Crippen in 1910.

Right: The Central Criminal Courts from Holborn Viaduct, *c.* 1920. This unusually angled view from St Sepulchre's church, left, hints at the grandeur of the 'Old Bailey' and its dome, topped by the statue of Justice.

Fire damage at No. 45 Cheapside by Bread Street. On 1 September 1881, a gas fitter at he premises of wine, spirit and tea merchants T. Foster & Co. recklessly tested for a gas leak on the first floor with a lighted candle in his hand. The resulting explosion and fire consumed the building in a spectacle which attracted crowds of onlookers and was visited by the Prince of Wales (later Edward VII) on the following day. The firm set up a temporary branch in St Paul's Churchyard during their rebuilding.

Whitefriars Fire Station, Carmelite Street, *c.* 1906. The ravages of fire have shaped the City through the centuries, but it was not until 1865 that the Metropolitan Board of Works established the Metropolitan Fire Brigade. Control of the brigade was taken over by the London County Council in 1889 and in 1904 there was a new name, the London Fire Brigade. The Gothic-styled fire station in Carmelite Street was begun in 1896 and is seen here as the earliest motorised appliances were appearing, this one with chains on its solid tyres to aid adhesion on the often slippery roads of Edwardian London.

The London Salvage Corps, near Mansion House, 1911. Working from headquarters in Watling Street, this separate salvage force was created in 1866 to rescue insured property at fires. This is one of the Salvage Corps' appliances as it returns to Watling Street from a fire in Phipp Street, Finsbury.

Above and left: City Police, *c.* 1912. While London beyond the City's boundaries is protected by the Metropolitan Police Force, the Square Mile has since 1839 had the unique distinction of possessing a force of its own, the City of London Police Force. Among the duties of the City's force is the policing of the vast crowds which descend on the Square Mile during its great celebrations, but on a more mundane level were the traffic control duties in an age before electric traffic lights took over much of this work. Both pictures are from a time when motor traffic was becoming more dominant; the unfortunate officer in the upper picture had a blizzard to contend with as well.

Fenchurch Street Station, *c.* 1912 (*above*); *c.* 1920 (*below*). The first railway terminus in the City, the London & Blackwall Railway's Fenchurch Street, opened in 1841 and was served by trains which were hauled by cable to Minories Station on the City boundary and the 'thrown off' the cable to reach Fenchurch Street under their own momentum. A gentle gradient allowed a return to Minories by gravity – steam trains did not arrive here until 1849. The new era of rail travel boosted the City's fortunes and ended much of the reliance on indifferent roads to connect with the rest of the country – London eventually had more main-line rail termini than any other capital city. Fenchurch street was rebuilt in 1935 and from 1983-87 new office blocks arose above it. The station's grand façade overlooking the forecourt (below) dates from 1854.

Liverpool Street Station, *c.* 1908. Built on the site of the Priory of St Mary Bethlehem which was founded in 1247, Liverpool Street Station was from 1875 the terminus of the Great Eastern Railway's lines, these having previously terminated at Bishopsgate Station in Shoreditch (see page 6). The photograph reveals the cluttered concourse of earlier years before the station was remodelled to give the bright, airy environment beneath preserved Victorian ironwork more familiar today.

Liverpool Street Station, *c.* 1920. The station is distinguished by its French Gothic-style architecture, the spirit of which was retained when the station was modernised from 1985-91.

Rush hour at Broad Street Station, *c.* 1920. The daily ritual of arrival and departure enacted at the North London Railway's City terminus which opened in 1865. Closure in 1984 left the site available for the innovative Broadgate, the largest private development in the City in post-war years. Liverpool Street station is on the right.

Holborn Viaduct Station, 1913. Opened in 1874, the platforms were on a viaduct above Fleet Lane and served passengers on the London, Chatham and Dover line. Although located on a busy main road, the station had a discreet profile, the lofty Holborn Viaduct Station Hotel (opened 1876) being a more impressive feature.

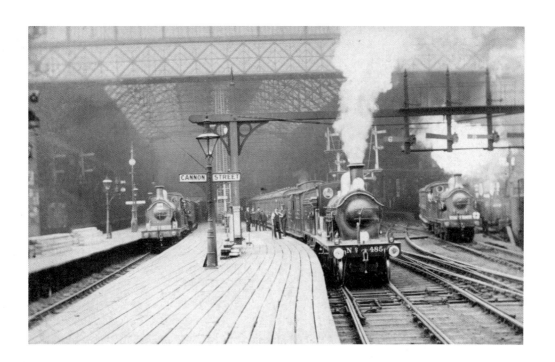

LONDON, Cannon Street, No. 1148.

Mansion House Underground Station and Cannon Street, *c.* 1920. On 10 January 1863 a small number of Londoners became the first paying passengers in the world to travel on a new kind of railway, one which ran beneath the congested streets of a major city. Initially the Metropolitan Railway ran from the then suburb of Paddington to the City at Farringdon Street, but the pioneering travellers on that first day could not have imagined that their short line would in time expand to become the greatest of all urban railways, the London Underground. Travelling conditions, however, were not ideal, the steam-driven locomotives adding their own aromas to the tunnels through which they ran, but from 1905 electrification of these sub-surface lines improved matters, and a new generation of electric deep-level Tube lines was already linking new parts of the capital into the Underground system. Mansion House Station, a multi-entranced facility opened for business on 3 July 1871 as the first stop on the District Railway's extension from Blackfriars. While the station was being built it was known as 'Cannon Street' but the familiar name prevailed upon opening to the public. The view is of the busy road junction with Queen Victoria Street, left and Cannon Street, centre, the church of St Mildred, Bread Street rising above the rooftops. With the exception of the distant St Paul's Cathedral, all the buildings seen here have been lost or rebuilt.

Opposite above: Cannon Street Station, *c.* 1910. Utilising the old site of the Hanseatic Merchant's Steelyard (see page 17), the South Eastern Railway's lines entered the City in style via a dedicated Thames bridge (1865). The terminus was spanned by a lofty arched roof between flanking walls featuring towers to reflect the City's architecture.

Opposite below: Cannon Street Station Hotel, *c.* 1880. Also built in 1865, the hotel's design was full of Victorian extravagance – a dull post-war office block is a poor replacement but a new building has been promised.

Aldersgate (Barbican) Station, c. 1918. The first stop on the eastward extension of the original section of the Metropolitan Railway was Aldersgate Street (1865), later called 'Aldersgate' and from 1968 'Barbican'. Great Northern Railway trains also used the station from 1866 – these lines were later used by Thameslink services. The view with its mixture of steam and electric trains shows the arched roof which was not replaced after war damage.

Moorgate Station, c. 1910. In the days before London's famous red, white and blue roundel came to symbolise much of the capital's public transport, some stations were almost hidden by a mass of route details while others adopted the discreet approach. Moorgate (1865) was one of these with two of its entrances barely visible among the shops of this typical City block.

The Central London Railway (Central Line), 1908. The new generation of deep-level electric Tube railways was a considerable advance upon the by now ageing steam Underground lines, and from 30 July 1900 Londoners could ride on the latest of them, the Central London Railway. With a flat fare of 2d, the longer journeys from Shepherds Bush to Bank were cheaper and far quicker than was possible on the old horse buses. This poster map shows the line's first extension, to White City for the Franco-British Exhibition in 1908.

Bank Station, St Mary Woolnoth, 1932. One of the curiosities of the City, Hawksmoor's mighty St Mary Woolnoth (1716-27) was the only London church to contain a Tube station. The City & South London Railway was London's first deep-level Tube (1890) with an extension to Moorgate via Bank, opening in 1900. Ingenious measures were needed to fit a station into a locality of historic buildings and limited space – the solution was the creation of a booking hall in the crypt of St Mary's. Nearby, a unique street sign proclaimed 'Station under the church opposite'.

Aldgate Tram Terminus, Whitechapel High Street, *c.* 1880. In the 1870s horse-drawn tramways were perceived as the future for London's street transportation, and with the City at the centre of a network of busy highways, tramway operators were anxious to include the Square Mile in their systems. They were, however, frustrated by the City's refusal to allow any trams onto its streets and were therefore obliged to terminate their lines as close to the City boundaries as possible. It was not until the early twentieth century that electric trams were allowed to cross the boundaries, but only for a few yards except on the Victoria Embankment where a through line was approved. The view is from the first decade of permanent tram operation in London (there had been earlier experiments) and pictures a lively scene at the North Metropolitan Tram Company's terminus close to the historic site of Aldgate Bars, an old entrance to the City. These new services offered a smoother ride to the City. These new services offered a smoother ride to the City from the eastern suburbs than had been possible on the older horse buses which had rough Victorian road surfaces to contend with. The terminus was a simple affair, just a pair of lines running into a short reversing track which allowed the horses to be unhitched and led to the opposite end of the tramcar for the return journey. The tramcar on the right had just arrived from distant Stratford while to the left, another prepares to return to Limehouse and Poplar. Aldgate was the City's principal eastern entry point with roads from East Anglia and the Thames-side docklands converging in the narrow High Street. The result was a cacophonous gridlock as every man and his horse fought for road space and the heavily laden hay wagons bound for Whitechapel Haymarket added to the melee. In the midst of it all, a bookseller trades from a roadside barrow, right.

Moorgate Street Tram Terminus, *c.* 1920. Moorgate's terminus handled passengers travelling to the City from northern suburbs including Hampstead and Highgate. The facility opened in 1871 with electric trams replacing the old horse-drawn services in 1907.

Holborn trolleybus terminus, Charterhouse Street, *c.* 1959. Drawing their power from overhead wires, trolleybuses were swift, silent and environmentally friendly, but they were a transport phenomenon which came and went with astonishing rapidity, lasting only around thirty years in London. Both services seen here ceased in January 1961 and London's last trolleybus ran in May 1962. (Courtesy D.A. Jones, London Trolleybus Preservation Society).

Horse buses in Fleet Street, June 1902. London without its buses would be unthinkable, yet before 1829 there were none. In that year, carriage builder George Shillibeer introduced London's first horse bus service on a route between Marylebone and the Bank of England. With Londoners liking the convenience of the new transport, other operators joined in and soon a network of bus services spread throughout the capital. Prominent in these early days were the London General Omnibus Co. who began their services in 1856 – this firm is the direct ancestor of London Transport and TfL of the present day. By the end of the nineteenth century there were so many horse buses on London's streets they created their own traffic jams, as here where the drivers fumed in a jam of their own making. This could sometimes work in the passenger's favour if the object of the ride was to indulge in some sightseeing – it has long been held that one of the best places to view London's passing panorama is from the top of a bus. June 1902 was a case in point and with the street decorated for the forthcoming Coronation of King Edward VII, everyone seen here seems content to enjoy the sights. Sadly, however, the King suffered a sudden illness, and the Coronation was postponed until 9 August 1902. In that year, fashion dictated that everyone shall wear a hat, even in high summer.

Threadneedle Street, Bank of England, *c*. 1920. It is 1920, the old horse buses have long gone and London has its first standardised fleet of red buses of the motor age, the renowned 'B' type. The red liveries of these 'General' buses had prevailed over the rainbow hues of earlier years when the colour of the bus denoted its route. Bank had been the terminus of London's first bus service, nearly a century earlier.

St Martin's-le-Grand from Newgate Street, *c*. 1920. The 3,000 strong 'B' type fleet dominated bus travel in London for around fifteen years, but as is seen here, the horse still had a place in the City's traffic.

Guildhall, *c.* 1900. Built from 1411–39 on part of a site once occupied by the amphitheatre of Roman London, Guildhall remains central to the City's civic life and a spectacular setting for grand City banquets. Although its fifteenth-century style prevails, some of what is seen above ground level was recreated in Victorian times, but below ground the undercroft retains much medieval masonry including remains of an even earlier Guildhall. The stone porch dating from 1788–89 is in a contrasting Oriental Gothic style, but the Victorians' desire to give Guildhall a more medieval appearance led to its partial removal (as seen here) only for it to be reinstated in 1910.

Above: Goldsmith's Hall, Foster Lane, *c.* 1908. Craft guilds representing the interests of various trades in the City were first recorded in the twelfth century and the Livery Companies we know today are descended from them. Robed Liverymen are a familiar presence at City events like the Lord Mayor's Show in which several of the Companies have floats which highlight their activities. The historic halls of the Livery Companies are scattered about the City – the Goldsmiths have occupied their hall since 1835 but have had a presence in Foster Lane since the 1300s. The term 'Hallmark' comes from the practice of marking the standard of precious metals at Goldsmith's Hall.

Right: Ironmonger's Hall, Fenchurch Street, *c.* 1910. The hall of the Worshipful Company of Ironmongers stood in Fenchurch Street since 1457 but the hall seen here which dated from 1745 was destroyed in an air raid in 1917. A picturesque new Ironmonger's Hall was built in 1925 off Aldersgate Street beside what is now the Museum of London.

The City from St Bride's, Fleet Street, *c.* 1905. It is only in the past fifty or so years that tall commercial blocks have begun to dominate the City skyline; before that it was the churches, the cathedral and the Monument which stood tallest giving wide-ranging views across the old low-rise City. St Bride's church boasts the loftiest spire of Wren's rebuilt churches and offers a panoramic outlook over the old valley of the river Fleet towards Holborn Viaduct, as seen here. Running diagonally along the lower part of the picture is St Bride Street, a road cut through in 1871 as part of the Holborn Viaduct improvements. Farringdon Street with its varied building styles and old pubs also shows up well with the Gothic Congregational Hall, right, which opened in 1875 on the site of ancient Fleet Prison. Also to the right is Holborn Viaduct Station and the substantial brick wall which is the rear of the station's hotel. Beyond are Smithfield and Farringdon Markets and at the far left is the tower of St Andrew Holborn, the largest of Wren's City churches. The site of St Bride's church is of considerable antiquity and its crypts contain masonry from Roman and Saxon periods.

Earl Street neighbourhood, Blackfriars, *c.* 1857. As ever, St Paul's commands the skyline, but more unusually this early photograph features one of the old neighbourhoods about to be swept away for the construction of Queen Victoria Street. Earl Street was a short road which linked Upper Thames Street with New Bridge Street and which contained an early headquarters of the British & Foreign Bible Society, left, an organisation set up in 1804 to further the spread of the Holy Scriptures worldwide. The society's grand new stone-fronted building was, in 1869, one of the first in the new Queen Victoria Street – it can still be seen although the society has since departed. Visible here is the tower of the Wren church of St Andrew-by-the-Wardrobe (1685–94) whose curious name comes from The Wardrobe, the Crown's stores department which stood nearby from the fourteenth century.

Other local titles published by Tempus

London Past and Present

MICHAEL BARRETT AND DOUGLAS WHITWORTH

London has seen vast changes since the end of the Second World War. By using a selection of evocative images from London in the Post-War Years by Douglas Whitworth, Michael Barrett compares them with modern scenes taken from similar viewpoints. The stunning colour photography captures the daily lives of residents, workers and visitors, creating an important visual record of England's capital city.

978 07524 4304 1

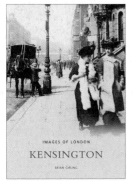

Kensington

BRIAN GIRLING

This fascinating selection of over 200 old photographs of the Royal Borough of Kensington shows a surprisingly varied range of activities and views from this unique area of London over a period of 100 years. Most of the images collected are published for the first time and have been drawn from the author's own extensive collection of old picture postcards.

978 07524 0369 4

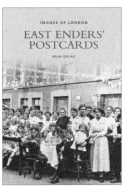

East Enders' Postcards

BRIAN GIRLING

This selection of old views from the capital city's East End combines popular sights with everyday scenes; from aerial views of Tower Bridge and London Docks to vistas of terraced houses, shops and businesses, as well as trams, streets and buildings which have long since disappeared. Images of King George V's Silver Jubilee celebrations in 1935, along with markets at Brick Lane, reflect the traditional community spirit for which this area of London is renowned.

978 07524 2494 1

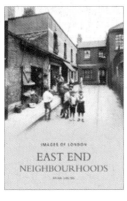

East End Neighbourhoods

BRIAN GIRLING

The River Thames with its docks, wharves and associated industries, has been a source of livelihood for generations of East Enders living in the historic riverside neighbourhoods of the former Metropolitan Borough of Stepney, Poplar and adjacent areas. East End Neighbourhoods draws on both private and public pictorial archives to offer a fascinating glimpse into the past of one of the most individual and fascinating quarters of London.

978 07524 3519 0

If you are interested in purchasing other books published by Tempus, or in case you have difficulty finding any Tempus books in your local bookshop, you can also place orders directly through our website

www.tempus-publishing.com